MERLIN CAROTHERS

VICTORY
ON PRAISE MOUNTAIN

Books by Merlin Carothers have now been translated and printed into thirty-one languages. Their unique and powerful messages have caused them to be distributed in sixty countries.

MERLIN CAROTHERS' praise books
include Prison to Praise, Power in Praise,
Answers to Praise, Praise Works!
Walking and Leaping, Bringing
Heaven Into Hell, The Bible on Praise
and More Power to You!

MERLIN CAROTHERS

VICTORY

ON PRAISE MOUNTAIN

MERLIN R. CAROTHERS
ESCONDIDO, CALIFORNIA 92025

The names of some persons
mentioned in this book
have been changed.

Contents

Preface

All my life I have worked for unity and harmony within any body with which I was associated, and would try to avoid dissension at all costs. But most of us will reach a time in life when we will have to stand up firmly for what we know is right. Two years ago, I had to, and became involved in a horrendous church fight. That will come as a surprise to many who have not heard about it (although as we lived through the media coverage of it and the hate mail and the phone campaign, it was difficult to conceive of anyone *not* hearing of it).

Throughout the episode, the Lord made it very clear to me that I was to stand silent, and let Him and the witness of His Holy Spirit be my defense. And they have. The only reason I feel His release to summarize it now, is to provide a brief and minimal background for the marvelous and miraculous things that He has done and is continuing to do in our body of believers, as He brings us into new maturity in Christ and new understanding of the origins and workings of spontaneous praise.

Before He can bring us into the promised land, He almost always needs to take us through the wilderness. When we are saved, we are taken out of Egypt and given a foretaste of the promised land. But in between, every one of us, it seems, needs to spend some time in the wilderness, learning, surrendering and growing. It took only a short while to get the Israelites out of Egypt, but forty years to get Egypt out of the Israelites. It needn't take us that long.

Needless to say, I did not realize any of this four years ago, when I wrote *Walking and Leaping*. Back then, we were at the pinnacle, and it seemed like we would keep on moving from height to height. It was as if we had passed through the portals of Egypt and directly into Canaan, with no indication that it would ever be otherwise.

Merlin R. Carothers
Escondido, California

November
1978

MERLIN CAROTHERS

VICTORY

ON PRAISE MOUNTAIN

CHAPTER • ONE

Onward and Upward

Easter Sunday morning, 1976, and the 1200-seat sanctuary of North County Christian Center was nearly full, for the first of our three services. I should have been brimming over with joy, but instead I was praying fervently for grace, discernment, and above all, wisdom. For I had a premonition that all the oppressive tension that had been building up during the past few months was about to explode.

Stepping to the lectern, I greeted the waiting congregation as cheerfully as I could. "Happy Easter!" And the congregation replied in kind. "Isn't this a glorious day?" And many glad "Amens" was the response.

And then behind me, I heard the whisper, "Let me speak now, Merlin." It was the eldest of our six associate pastors. I shook my head no.

"I demand that you give me that microphone now, Merlin!" he hissed, but again I shook my head.

"I will not be silenced!" he exclaimed, and as I watched, transfixed, he strode to the edge of the platform and began shouting at the congregation: *"Merlin Carothers is a dictator! He runs this church like he thinks he's God! He. . . ."* On and on the litany went, at the top of his voice. I couldn't breathe, and felt like I had been kicked in the stomach by a mule. And the congregation, stunned, bewildered and ultimately disgusted, began to leave in twos and threes and then in throngs. By the time his forty-five-minute tirade subsided, there was hardly anyone left in church.

I could not believe what had just happened, and on Easter Sunday! But it was nothing to the horrors that lay ahead.

Have things ever gone so well for you that you didn't see how God could bless you more than He already had? Has your heart ever been overflowing with praise and thanksgiving, and suddenly God pours out still more blessings on you?

Enjoy them! Your surprise and wonder delights your heavenly Father's heart. But take care, lest you unconsciously fall into the assumption that such bliss will continue unbroken until the Lord's return. For that is not the way God works. We are put on this earth to praise Him not only with our lips but in our lives. We are also put here to grow and mature that we may be deepened and conformed more to His image. The way to spiritual maturity is often one of stormy and painful interludes.

In the Christian's path, there are, unquestionably, high mountain meadows, sunbathed and adorned with wildflowers, where soft grasses wave in a gentle breeze, and a spring-fed brook runs beside a tall, broad-limbed tree. These are places of incredible beauty, where the Lord would have us rest and refresh ourselves. Drink of the cool water, lie down in the shade of the tree, and doze. But don't put your pack and your walking shoes too far away, because the path leads onward and upward, and ahead may lie narrow, treacherous places, the likes of which you have never imagined, even rockslides that would hurl you from the path.

Let me back up a little before that unforgettable Easter service. Thanksgiving Sunday, 1975—the organ was just concluding one of our favorite praise choruses, as I entered the sanctuary and took my place on the raised platform that defined the altar area of our church. Smoothly the organ shifted to the melody of a traditional Thanksgiving hymn, and I looked out over the packed congregation. It seemed to me that the gratitude I saw reflected on those beaming faces was indeed heartfelt. We all knew how much we had to be grateful for.

Closing my eyes for a moment, I drifted back over the past three years, to when Mary and I and the children had first arrived in the Southern California hill town of Escondido, which means "Hidden Valley," to help start a new church. That first Sunday, as I stepped up to preach in Del Dios Junior High, I had looked over the lectern at twenty-five faces, and had found it difficult to praise God. Many

3

of these same people had been meeting together for the previous six years under the leadership of the elder associate pastor who had invited me to come, and still they numbered no more than these twenty-five on a Sunday morning. At forty-seven, I had burned all my bridges, giving up a beautiful, growing church in Indiana, and a lovely new parsonage, to say nothing of my Methodist minister's pension, and accepted a pastor's position that had no home and no salary, nor any promise of one. In fact, there was no promise of anything, except a free hand as senior pastor to be in charge of everything connected with the church, though at the moment there was not a whole lot to be in charge of.

But God had called me to Southern California and intended to raise up a new work there; that much I was convinced of. And so I praised Him that morning with my lips, though in my heart there was anxiety and doubt. And then, as I stood there, the Lord reminded me that in the beginning my congregation in Indiana, the first since my retirement as a lieutenant colonel in the army chaplaincy, had been no larger than this one. *Practice what you preach*, God's words formed in my heart. *Praise me now for these twenty-five souls. Carry out each assignment that I give you to the best of your ability, and I will provide the increase.*

Chagrined, I did. And He did. The next Sunday, there were fifty worshipers, and the Sunday after that, nearly a hundred. Many were coming because they had read my books, but a number were also coming because they had been asking God where to worship, and He had brought them. In three short years, He raised up a magnificent plant and was still increasing it. We had just purchased thirty-nine more acres and were drawing up plans for a new church, for we had already outgrown our present one. Its seating capacity was only 1200, which meant that we had to have three morning services to accommodate the more than two thousand worshipers who came every Sunday. Many enjoyed the services so much that they stayed on for two services every Sunday. Our new, two-story addition housed another twenty classrooms, which were just barely enough to handle our Sunday school classes, Junior Church, and nursery. We had a prayer tower, with volunteers manning phones around the clock, taking prayer requests and offering counsel to callers from all over the country.

North County Christian Center was a place of constant activity, whether it was women's Bible studies during the day, or evening meetings which were blocked out for the whole week. On Tuesday nights, the deacons, elders, Sunday school teachers, and missionaries had their meeting; Wednesdays, we had family Bible studies; Thursdays, outside speakers came, and I was proud that North County had become a "name" church that attracted the best-known Christian speakers in the country; Fridays, Michael Esses, a Jewish believer and scholar came down from Melodyland Christian Center to conduct well-attended seminars on the Old Testament; Saturday night was youth night; Sunday evening was really just a carry-over from Sunday morning, more informal, and with the emphasis on sharing, rather than a sermon. We tried to leave Mondays open, to give people a rest, but invariably that was the night we had all the meetings that couldn't be fitted in to any of the other evenings.

Our parking lot held four hundred cars and was expanding all the time. The asphalt filled up quickly on Sunday morning, and people parked on the dirt next to it. When, after a while, the dirt became packed down, we would simply pave over it, and the process would continue. It had to, for ours was a mobile congregation: on Sunday, three to four hundred people drove up from San Diego twenty-five miles to the southwest, and a dozen or so people would drive down from Los Angeles, ninety miles north. Weekly, we would even have people fly in for the service, from places like Las Vegas.

North County's membership was a pretty loose thing, and we prided ourselves on how "free in the Spirit" we were. If a person who had been coming fairly regularly felt like he or she was a member, well, then, they were. And that was all there was to it. Some visitors on vacation were so moved by the love they felt there that they wanted to join, even though their home church was thousands of miles away. We encouraged this, and also welcomed any worshipers from the local area who wanted to drop in on one of our earlier services, before going to their own churches. In these instances, I made a strong point (and still do) of encouraging them to stay in their churches and serve God there, rather than leaving them to join ours, though they were always welcome to continue coming and praising God with us, too.

The Thanksgiving hymn ended, and I came out of my reverie, looking at Mary down in the front row, with Bruce who was fifteen now, and Genie, who was eleven. They grinned up at me, and Genie waved, and I felt tears come to my eyes. How could we ever begin to thank God for all that He had done for us in these past three years? My own national ministry, the Foundation of Praise, had been officially incorporated only a few months before, yet was already well embarked on fulfilling God's foremost call on my life: to spread the message of praise as far as possible. The main thrust of our foundation was to get the praise books into prisons, and it had been a long uphill struggle. Wardens and chaplains who didn't know of the books were reluctant to help us, even hostile. But wherever the books were accepted, they were often the instruments God used to reach the embittered, and many prisoners experienced profound and lasting spiritual changes in their lives. In fact, so radical was the change in such cases that often chaplains would call to tell us of the fantastic—and sincere—reversal of so-and-so's behavior, and could we possibly send more books. Men who had been sentenced to prison for murder and had then perhaps murdered another prisoner, were being transformed by the amazing power of one small book.

The previous year, we had received a tremendous encouragement from the Lord. A Christian friend named Herb Ellingwood, who was the legal secretary to Governor Reagan, persuaded the governor to approve having *Prison to Praise* in every prison in California. I had not realized, at first, what a significant boost this was, but where before we had been urging the wardens to take our books, now wardens and state officials from all over California were calling and requesting them. Two officials even drove to our home in Escondido to pick them up.

The incidents of remarkable conversions in the state prisons increased, so much so, that word began to travel to other states, and before long we began receiving book requests from prisons we had never heard of. As of that Thanksgiving, we had given away more than 100,000 copies of the praise books (and as of this writing, that figure is now more than 500,000). We had an office with four full-time staffers, kept busy processing reports sent in by joyful people of what had happened to them when they put the praise principle to work and started praising God, regardless of circumstances. Accounts of physical, mental and spiritual healings abounded, and we tried to share as many as possible in a monthly newsletter to our supporters, who then numbered around twelve thousand.

As often as possible, I would spread the praise message in person, flying to speak wherever invited—in prisons, churches, or Full Gospel Business Men's Meetings. I was usually able to accept one or two of the thirty invitations a week that came in, but I tried not to be gone more than two or three days, and never on Sunday. As it was, there were times when I felt that I was losing the close touch that a pastor should have with what is going on in his church, but I relied on the six associate pastors, seven elders, and fifty deacons to bring to my attention any matter that needed my direct concern. As long as I was there to preach on Sunday and coordinate every new program, I felt that I was doing my part, and thus far everything had gone incredibly smoothly.

And our reputation was growing. Pastors from other states were coming to see for themselves, and marveling that at last they had found the "ideal New Testament church."

With a start, I realized that the organist was waiting for me to open the Thanksgiving service. And so I stood and thanked God, on behalf of all of us, for the bountiful increase he had so lavishly bestowed upon us in the past year, and I asked Him to help us to remember whence it came, and what we were before we learned to praise Him. It was a joyous service, with much spontaneous hand-clapping and laughter during the singing, which was exactly the way I liked it.

That Thanksgiving service was memorable, mainly because of so many grateful hearts. I didn't know when it had ever been so easy to praise God, as it was that morning. We seemed to go from height to height, and there was no reason to suspect that it would ever be otherwise.

But on this clear blue horizon, a cloud was forming. Actually, it had been there a long time, only so small that no one had noticed it. Especially me, who, in what can only be called deliberate naivete, had dismissed any nudges the Holy Spirit had given me that all was not as it should be.

God's love was so great and so fully demonstrated at North County, that it was more than sufficient to cover any ripples that might emerge. But now the cloud had grown clearly visible, and I ignored it at my peril and the peril of my flock. A storm was coming for anyone who had eyes to see it, but I kept my rose-colored glasses firmly in place.

CHAPTER • TWO

The Storm Breaks

The first rumble of distant thunder was heard in the early spring of 1976. The North County church was growing so fast that we had scarcely time to catch our breath, let alone make concrete plans for the future. We did have one pressing need, a new church building. And although it seemed utterly inconceivable to me that we would require a seating capacity of four thousand, friends pointed out that that had been my attitude, when it was proposed that we expand our present capacity from eight hundred to twelve hundred. "You keep preaching God's message, pastor," one had said to me, "and God will bring the people. Don't be surprised if four thousand isn't enough!" Well, I contented myself, at least it would not be built until the Lord provided the funds.

But now the suggestion was made by our elder associate pastor that we should develop a retirement community, so that people from all across America could come and be a part of North County, helping to build the church in their retirement years. When the proposal was initially made by Ernie, I liked the sound of it, for I felt we should be reaching out a helping hand to everyone, the old as well as the young. And so I said that while it was obviously not something that we should implement right away, it might indeed fit into our plans somewhere in the future, and I suggested that a committee of half a dozen men from the church be asked to consider it.

With that, I put the proposal for a retirement community out of mind. And there it stayed, until the committee's preliminary investigation revealed that an enormous amount of money would be needed, just to get the project off the ground—some $900,000! Furthermore, Ernie proposed that the way to raise the money was to sell bonds to the members of the church. At that point, I withdrew my support completely. Ours was not a wealthy congregation, and a number of families had already gone into personal debt, to help raise the money to build our present church. It did not witness to me that we should go to them so soon again, and for such a large sum.

But apparently I did not make my disapproval sufficiently clear. For when I came back from one of my speaking engagements, I discovered that while I was away, Ernie had contacted a professional bond-raising company and arranged for them to make a presentation to the committee of how they would go about raising the bonds from our people. I sat in on that meeting, and was inwardly repelled by the intensive, high-pressure methods of raising funds that were being discussed. This was not at all in keeping with the way we had been doing things at North County!

And yet, I didn't speak. The six men on the committee seemed to have no objection. And besides, perhaps God did want to move in this direction. But I felt I had to at least put a caution out, and so I said we really needed to wait carefully upon the Lord now, and consider the whole thing with much prayer before we took any further steps. Also, we had reached the point where we now needed to put the proposal before the congregation and have the benefit of their input before proceeding. And once again, I put it out of mind.

I shouldn't have. A week or so later, returning from another speaking engagement, I discovered that while I was gone, Ernie had independently signed a contract with the bond-raising company and had paid them an advance of $5000. On checking with the members of the committee, I found that every one of them had had the same check in his spirit that I had; the reason they had not spoken was because they had gotten the impression from Ernie that I was *for* the project!

That evening, atop the foothill where our house is located, I talked the entire situation through with Mary, after our children had gone to bed. It was a warm night, so we sat outside and watched the stars come out over Escondido. I saw that it was my own fault that things had been allowed to go this far. If I had just spoken out how I felt right at the beginning, if I had asked the others to say how they really felt—but instead, I had wanted to avoid hurting people's feelings. I had obviously not exercised the leadership I should have, and now, because of my ducking that dilemma, we faced an even larger one: the church had incurred a contractural obligation. As Christians, what kind of a witness would it be, if we now tried to back out of our commitment?

For hours, Mary and I talked and prayed. We did not want to stand in God's way, if the project truly was His will, and yet we could not gain any peace whatsoever about the whole situation. In the end, it seemed that the only possible course open to us was for me to immediately call a meeting of the board of directors and offer to resign from the board and the pastorate, if the board or the church felt strongly that the retirement project was God's plan for the present.

The meeting took place in my office the following morning, and the board was shocked that I would even consider resigning. None of them, except Ernie, thought the project had merit, and even Ernie said that it would be wise to set it aside for the time being. And so the project was tabled indefinitely, and the $5000 was subsequently returned. But from that point on, there was a marked cooling in Ernie's attitude toward me, though we had been the closest of friends for three years. I did everything in my power to effect a reconciliation. Repeatedly rebuffed, I counted on time, the abundance of God's love which surrounded us, and all the exciting things He was doing in our midst to work a change in our relationship.

But that was not to be the case. Time had no opportunity to work a healing; less than a week after the retirement project had been set aside, a serious moral situation that had been going on between a part-time member of our staff and a member of our congregation was brought to my attention. Not that we were a legalistic church; if anything, we went out of our way to be sensitive and compassionate in all situations. But there were certain actions that in God's eyes were absolutely wrong, and Scripture was clear and explicit on them. To the associate pastors and the board of directors, I pointed out that if we were serious about following the Lord, we were bound to observe His laws for right behavior. Some action would have to be taken.

Ernie challenged this, saying that he had looked into the situation himself, and it didn't seem so serious and would probably resolve itself if we overlooked it. He threatened to get up publicly and denounce me as a dictator if we took any action. And so, against my better judgment and since that was what most of the others decided was best under the circumstances, we did nothing.

Less than a week passed before another moral situation, more serious than the first, came to light.

And now I knew that I could not back down. I called a meeting of the directors and pastors, and said that as long as I was pastor of North County Christian Center, I could not condone or turn a blind eye to grave moral wrongdoing taking place on our staff.

Without warning, Ernie exploded! "Merlin Carothers is a dictator!" he screamed. "He is trying to ram his authority down our throats!" On and on he went, shaking off the other pastors' and directors' attempts to calm him down. Too stunned and horrified to speak, I waited until his shouting subsided, then got up and left, as did the others present. There was nothing else to do. I felt sick, never having experienced anything like this before. But the worst was yet to come.

It came Easter Sunday. I still do not know how I got through that day. When it was over, I said to Mary, "All I want to do is get out. I still can't believe it actually happened. These last few weeks are like some ghastly nightmare, only I can't wake up; it just keeps going on and on."

Mary shook her head. "I can't believe it either. When we first came here, I thought of him as my father; I even took to calling him 'Dad.' But I've been praying about it, and the only thing that comes to me is, 'Stand still, and see the salvation of the Lord' " (Exod. 14:13).

We were sitting out on our patio again, and I looked at her, amazed. The same words had been coming to me, and earlier that same day, two other

16

friends had come to me and said that they had gotten the same verse!

The "still" part, I could certainly buy; from the moment Ernie had first begun his attacks, I had received a strong word from the Lord to remain silent before my accuser and make no reply whatsoever. But did "stand" mean remain in the church? Everything in me wanted to leave this horrible situation, to get as far away from it as I possibly could, and as fast as possible. I had invitations to be pastor of several larger churches, and in one of them at twice the salary I was receiving at North County. But would that be fair to all those whom the Lord had given me responsibility for? There was already so much chaos and confusion in the wake of what had happened, that I felt I could not abandon them.

Then too, as in the beginning of any such nightmare situation, there was always the hope that it really was like a bad dream, and that somehow, miraculously, all would be restored to its former peace and unity. And I was as human as the next person, when it came to wishful thinking. So I resolved to stand, and do everything I possibly could to heal the division and avoid any further dissension.

And I knew where to begin: on my knees, asking the Lord to search my heart and show me all the places where I had been wrong. He showed me quite a bit. Though His first call on my life was to a world-wide ministry of spreading the praise message, He had also subsequently called me to accept the pastorate of North County when it was offered, and to help build the church. Up until recently, there had never been any conflict between the two calls.

But now I could see that I had sorely neglected many of a pastor's traditional responsibilities. I had never even once asked to see the corporation papers of the church, had never in four years asked to see the church's financial records. I had trusted Ernie so much that I left all financial matters in his hands. In fact, I didn't even know what happened to the money, after the collection had been taken. All I knew was that Ernie kept it securely locked in a safe in his office. Volunteers helped him count the offering on Monday morning, but he kept the only records. It seemed hard to believe, in retrospect, that anyone could have been so naive, but there had always been enough money for the church's needs, and I just didn't think about it. The same thing went for taking enough time with each of the individual members of the congregation. I had relied on the associate pastors, elders and deacons to do that, but now I came to see that some two thousand souls were looking to me for spiritual leadership.

In other words, as long as the system seemed to be working, I simply hadn't concerned myself about it. But now there was plenty to be concerned about, and I asked the Holy Spirit to show me where else I had failed in my pastoral responsibility. Immediately, the guest speakers came to mind. We had had a steady parade of nationally prominent speakers through North County, and to be perfectly honest—as I had to be, under the Holy Spirit's searchlight—many of them had preached messages contradictory to one another, and some were even in conflict with the spirit of the praise message. No wonder there was often confusion in the wake of these speakers, as our flock was exposed to the voices of so many different shepherds! Now I had to face the fact that it was my pride in being a "name" church that had blinded me in this area.

Well, from now on, I would prayerfully consider each proposal for a visiting speaker as well as start paying close attention to the details of church administration and, as much as possible, the needs of the members. I had enjoyed the title of head pastor; it was about time I started earning it.

But the situation had deteriorated even further than I realized. Ernie was talking to the news media now, and all of Southern California was being made aware of our problems. Finally, things reached the point where the people simply had to be told what was going on, as most of them still didn't know. So I invited anyone who wanted to discuss the problem openly or ask any questions to meet with me in the fellowship hall one Friday in May.

About three hundred showed up, and before I began, I had a strange leading from the Lord. I asked if there were any present who did not intend to let me speak without interrupting me or preventing me. Seven hands went up. I then asked how many would give me a chance to say what I had to say and would see that I got it, using whatever means necessary. All the other hands went up.

So I began, carefully explaining everything that had happened, the steps that had been taken, and how I still firmly believed that God could bring complete healing to every member of our body—and would, if we cooperated with His leading. Nearly everyone seemed to be satisfied and ready to move forward. But as we left, there were, I noticed, still a handful of faces that were filled with hate. They were so few, I discounted them, but I was not then aware of what a few determined people could do.

The next thing I did was to go to the leadership of the church—the directors, elders and pastors—and told them of all the places that the Lord had shown me where I had failed them. I asked them to please show me any I had missed. To my surprise, nearly all of them were emphatic in their encouragement and support. But Ernie remained adamant, and it finally began to dawn on me that nothing short of my departure would ever satisfy him.

But as much as I wanted to leave, even more than that, I wanted to be obedient to God, and I did not yet have God's permission to go. So I stayed, and the nightmare went on.

Realizing that I now had to exercise my role as

shepherd, and sensing that something was very wrong with the way the church's funds were being handled, I asked the directors to appoint a new treasurer to replace Ernie. They appointed one of the most respected laymen of the church. Shortly after his appointment, he discovered that his inquiries confirmed my fears. Substantial funds had been misappropriated.

About this time the suggestion was made that all present members of the board resign, and that the church elect a new board, one that would be the chief authority in the church. I was tremendously relieved. Here, at last, would be the end of our problems!

To ensure a fair election, two pastors and one Christian attorney from other churches in the area came to act as impartial observers and to oversee the election for us.

On the evening of the election most of the local church members came and voted, and out of many nominations, seven men were duly elected. From that moment on, all authority in the church was to be in their hands. Hallelujah! I believed that God would use these men to determine the future direction of North County Christian Center, and I was delighted to submit to their decisions. The first time I met with them, I offered to stay and support them, or to resign and let them appoint a new senior pastor. And I indicated that the recent dissension might very well be God's way of saying that it was time I left. They all felt that I should stay.

But our problems were not over. They only entered the next phase. One of the first matters the new board addressed itself to was the fact that the church's finances had been under the exclusive control of Ernie. No one had ever seen the records—not even the new treasurer. The directors asked Ernie to bring them all the records so they could examine every aspect of the church financial history. He refused.

In the ensuing weeks, the pressure on the directors became so great that one of them simply resigned. Of the six remaining, five supported me and were urging me to take the whole matter of leadership to a church vote, assuring me that 90 percent of the congregation was solidly behind me. But if there was one thing I abhorred, it was the prospect of a gloves-off church fight, with the inevitable split and recriminations that would follow. So I asked all who accepted my leadership to do nothing that would precipitate it and urged them to pray for God's perfect will to be done.

And now came the worst time of all, beyond my darkest imaginings. Encouraged by our silence, the opposition became more vociferous than ever, calling in the media, who were attracted by the carnival atmosphere and responded enthusiastically. I continued my policy of making no comment and asked my supporters to do the same, but the reporters found Ernie and some of his friends more than willing to give interviews to any and all comers. In addition, a phone campaign was launched against me, and friends of mine in Christian leadership across the country were called and told the most incredible things. All told, by the estimate of several supporters, there weren't more than thirty-five or forty people actively involved in the anti-Carothers movement, but from the sound and fury they were generating, one would have thought there were ten times that number.

At this point, some friends suggested that if I wouldn't force a showdown, I could at least sue Ernie for libel. But the Lord had said, *Stand silent before your accusers*, and He had not released me from that stricture. Besides, the world's courts were no place for Christians to seek redress for inter-church grievances.

During all of this, it will come as no surprise that I was having a little trouble praising God with all my heart. I did it, nonetheless, and I knew He was in charge; but it perplexed me that things seemed to get progressively worse.

In many ways, one of the most painful experiences was to see what happened to a number of people who we had been confident would stand with us, come what may. They simply left the church. Or they would ask us to refute in detail every charge that had been laid against us. As patiently as I could, I would explain, and then explain all over again to the next person who asked, and then again, and again. But inside, my heart was breaking—physically as well as spiritually, it seemed. Though no one but Mary knew about it, I began having pains in my chest, and a check-up revealed that my heart was skipping beats. The doctors ordered me to rest, but how could anyone rest in a situation like ours?

I should say that to counterbalance our being abandoned by our assumed friends, it turned out that we had a number of staunch supporters among people we would never have expected to stand by us. That was indeed a cheering discovery and the whole process was a revelation to me of just how much we truly needed to be deepened and matured. Too many of us fail to appreciate that our Christian walk is not going to be just joy and fellowship. If it is to be at all effective for the Lord, then Satan is going to be active. We will have to engage in spiritual warfare, just as serious Christians always have. And yet, as I thought of those who chose to avoid all conflicts, if possible, and stay focused on the joy, I realized how much it had been my own nature to do the same. How I would have given anything to avoid the one I was in!

In June of '76, due to a commitment I had made months before, Mary and I had to be gone for a week, to lead a spiritual retreat. But being physically removed from the scene provided no relief; the new directors called me every day for advice. On the third day, they told me that now Ernie was accusing *them* of being dictators! Each one of them loved the church, but each was considering resigning his membership, because the spirit of antagonism was so great. I appealed to them to stand fast, and they agreed.

The next day they called to say that a guest speaker whom Ernie had invited was now speaking out against them and me, and when they had admonished him for this, he told them that he had already been informed that they were trying to be dictators. The directors then urged me to be at the church on the coming Friday night, to join them in explaining to the church what the latest controversy was all about, and I agreed to be home in time to be with them.

But when the five directors and I entered the church that Friday evening, we found the pulpit area completely encircled by two dozen of Ernie's cohorts, standing shoulder to shoulder, completely blocking our path. And it was clear that they had no intention of letting us pass.

I was angry then, more angry than I had ever been in my life. I started resolutely toward the pulpit, with the five directors around me. And then the Lord stopped me in my tracks.

Son, is this the way I have taught you?

But, Lord! What they're doing is wrong!

Look in your heart.

All the weeks of turning the other cheek, of being slandered and verbally spat upon and remaining silent, of the malicious hurt that had been done to my family and to those who had stood by us—my heart thirsted for vengeance. I am not a violent man by nature; if anything, I tend to be the opposite. Each of the ninety parachute jumps I had made with the 82nd Airborne had taken more prayer than the one before. But that night, the Lord was right; I was consumed with rage.

"Go on, Merlin!" one of my supporters whispered, interrupting my thoughts. "There are ten times as many of us, who will gladly clear the way for you! In fact, we've been waiting a long time for this!"

Suddenly, I could see the chaos and mayhem that was only a moment away. I looked down at my hands; they were clenched into fists, my knuckles white and trembling.

Taking a deep breath, I turned and walked slowly out of the church. And over seven hundred of the eight hundred present followed me.

Close behind me was my son-in-law, Lee, and my 6'3", 270-pound son, Carl, who had insisted on staying close to me during recent visits to the church, for fear that physical harm might befall me. I had chafed at Carl's concern, telling him that God would provide my protection, but he would just laugh and say, "That's right, He is. And I'm it." But that evening, when one of our most soft-spoken associate pastors lingered for a moment to try and make some sort of peace, one of the opposition came up and hit him, knocking him to the floor. After that, Mary announced, "Carl is staying with you, whether you like it or not!"

One final scene remained to be played. The next night, youth night, we received a report that the opposition had chained the doors of the church shut from the inside, to prevent the elected directors from speaking there. It was obvious to me that if that were the case, there would also be chains on the doors the next morning, Sunday morning. So I called a meeting of the directors, and the five who supported me came. There weren't many options left. Again, I offered to resign, but they refused to hear of it, reminding me of all the people who looked to me for spiritual leadership. And then one of them hit upon a solution so simple and ingenious that we knew it had to be the Holy Spirit: "Why don't we hold church in another location? After all, all we're talking about is a couple of buildings. The church *is* the people. If we can't use the buildings, then we'll simply have church where we can."

"What are you saying then?" I asked.

"We will get on the phone tonight and call people and let them know that we will be meeting somewhere else tomorrow morning."

"You're sure this is the only way? We will be charged with causing a church split."

"Look, Merlin," one of them said, "we know how much you are against a church split, but honestly, this is not what this is. We *are* the church's leadership, and our people will be hurt more now by remaining in the spirit that prevails in those buildings than by worshiping elsewhere."

Someone else spoke: "As your board of directors and spiritual head, we could tell you to do this, but we don't want to force you to do something against your own leading. Let it suffice that it is our strong and unanimous recommendation that we hold services elsewhere tomorrow. And for as long as the buildings remain closed to us."

I said nothing, and finally nodded, but I could not keep the tears from my eyes. For I had just remembered that Sunday morning in October, three years before, when I had walked into the brand new North County Christian Center, which so many had given so much to build. I had been wondering what would be the first thing I should say at our opening service. As I entered the back door, the Lord spoke to me: *Son, take off your shoes. You're standing on holy ground.* I had called the congregation to do the same, and they had. And now, I might never cross the threshold of North County again.

"Hey," said one of the directors cheerfully, "where are we going to meet? It's nearly ten o'clock now; we'll never be able to line up a school auditorium this late at night."

They thought a moment, and then someone said, "I know! We'll meet in Felicita Park!"

"Outside? In a park?"

"Sure, why not? Parks are for the public, aren't they?"

And with that, they went home, to start making calls.

CHAPTER • THREE

A New Thing

Sunday morning, July 26, 1976, 11:00 A.M.—the congregation of more than seven hundred was already in place, waiting expectantly, while the organ and piano played softly in the background. Only their place was not in the plush pews of North County. Their place was under the shade trees of Felicita Park, gathered on the grassy slopes and gentle knolls, and the instruments playing in the background were portables—miraculously sought out and borrowed, complete with a portable sound system.

It was a glorious morning! Above, the sky was a clean-washed blue, and the sun was streaming down in shafts through the limbs of the trees, just as softly as if it were filtering through stained-glass windows. Indeed, it was as if we were assembled in a beautiful open-air cathedral. Perhaps it was just my imagination, but it seemed to me that a special radiance filled the park. I do not know what the Shekinah glory of the Lord looks like, but I just may have been catching a glimpse of it that morning. Everything seemed so freshly scrubbed—as if it had been made ready for us—that I had no trouble imagining angels in our midst, ready to join in our praise.

We sang a few of our favorite choruses, and then I prayed, asking God to guide our feet each step of the way, and hold us in the hollow of His hand, as we entered joyously into His wilderness. And then we sang a hymn, "All Hail the Power of Jesus' Name," and the joy that burst forth from our hearts was unlike anything I had ever experienced in group worship! That hymn seemed to lift us two inches off the grass we stood on! The people were so happy to be able to worship in a peaceful atmosphere, free from the tension we had lived with for so many weeks, that there were tears of joy in many eyes as we sang.

What a blessed scene! We had no facilities for Junior Church or Sunday school, of course, so the older children stayed with their families, and the younger ones played quietly on the ground, on the periphery of our gathering. Some families had brought blankets to sit on, and some of the grandparents had brought folding chairs. There were a great many picnic hampers in evidence; many families obviously planned to make a day of it and just stay in the park until it was time for the evening service. It was all so peaceful and natural. For a moment I imagined that it might have been something like the earliest gatherings of followers at the feet of the Master.

"Your pastors would each like to share a little of what is on their hearts today," I said, "and before they do, I would just like to say that there is no bitterness in my heart. I just wish that we were *all* here and I hope that each one of you feels that same way." And the congregation signified their agreement by softspoken yet heartfelt "Amens."

Then, one by one, the four associate pastors who came with us shared the joy in their own hearts, and I found that I really did wish that Ernie and the others were with us.

And then the Lord spoke to us in a strong, clear word of prophecy: *Rejoice, because I am with you, and I am leading you, and these are glorious days. I have called you out, because I am doing a new thing. Be glad, therefore, and encourage one another, and continue to praise and pray. . . .*" As these last words died away, there was thunderous applause and even a few cheers, and many people wept tears of rejoicing. It had been the first time in months that the Lord had spoken to us through prophecy in our public meetings. And for the next several weeks, we were to receive prophetic encouragement at almost every meeting.

We were not sure whether it was legal to take an offering in the park, so we dispensed with it, but many of the people had such gratitude in their hearts that they sought out the directors and gave them their offerings anyway. It was early afternoon before the service was finally over, and many of the single people had not thought to bring anything to eat, so families with hampers just naturally asked them to join with them, thus starting a tradition of sharing with one another that has continued to this day.

At the close of the service, I announced that we didn't know where we would be meeting the following week, so would everyone please leave their names, addresses and telephone numbers on pads that were being circulated, and they would be called or receive a postcard. As I did so, I was reminded of the Christians behind the Iron Curtain who often had to keep moving their meetings, to avoid persecution. In many cases, I had heard, they simply had to rely on the Holy Spirit to direct them to the right place. (Ironically, we have moved so many times ourselves since then that quite often it's the Holy Spirit who directs new visitors to our meetings even now!) Someday, we Christians here might have to depend on Him in the same way, but at the moment I praised God for our telephones and our freedom of assembly.

The rest of the afternoon passed quickly; it was like an impromptu church picnic in the park! And in the evening service, one couple after another got up to share their joy. As I had hoped, there was no rancor towards those who had opposed us, no bitterness or hurt. They were forgiven, and the past was in the past.

As it turned out, we continued to meet in the park

for about two months, then in the Central School in Escondido, and presently in the Miller School. I wondered if, after the novelty of our new circumstances wore off, the amazing joy we all felt would die away. Would people have second thoughts? Would they begin to resent having given up such a magnificent tabernacle? Especially those who were still paying on loans which they had taken out to pay for North County? These were not wealthy people; it had cost them sacrifically to build that church. And what of those who had given so much of their time and talent to make North County's grounds and appointments so beautiful? All that loving care they had invested, and now they would never see it again. Surely, one could hardly blame them, if they were tempted to look back.

But to my knowledge, no one ever did. Instead, we were under tremendous grace, for our praise never diminished as the weeks turned into months. We knew we were where God wanted us to be, whether it was in a park or a school or even a movie theatre (which we had also investigated). And knowing that God was leading us, it didn't matter to us where he took us. Ours was a moveable feast, and our journey through the wilderness was a happy one.

I think it was our second Sunday in the park that someone came up to me and asked, "Merlin, it's obvious we're a church, even if we don't have a church building, but what are we going to call ourselves?"

Without thinking, I smiled and replied the first words that came into my head: "Praise Center."

I liked the sound of it, and the more I thought about it, the more appropriate it sounded. Well, of course! We were to be a center of praise, a place where people could come and learn with us what it meant to put praise into practice in one's daily life! And they would learn not just through teaching, but hopefully through the example of our daily lives. Because, as I thought about it, our corporate call as a united body was to praise God not only with our lips but *in our lives*. By the quality of our life, by the degree to which we had overcome self and were truly living in and for Him—this was how we would praise Him! A center of praise—thank you, Lord.

In the days that followed, I was intrigued to observe the many different ways God went about molding us into one body with a deeper commitment to Him, and to one another, than we had ever experienced before. For instance, we obviously had no place where we could meet during the week, yet still desirous of having as much fellowship together as we could, we were at a loss for a solution. And then it came to us: one family could invite three or four other families to come to their home each week, for dinner and an evening of prayer, Bible study and fellowship. So, every Wednesday, among those families who signed up, one family would bring a casserole to the home they were meeting in, another would bring a salad, and another a dessert, and they would break bread together and share what the Lord was doing in their lives. These family dinners or "pot-luck groups," as tney came to be called, would also each invite one or two single people, as well as a visiting couple who might be staying in town, just the way we had on that first Sunday in the park.

The pot-luck groups succeeded beyond our fondest hopes. For the first time in all the years that we had known one another, we were actually becoming involved in one another's lives, praying for one another, sharing problems and concerns, becoming, in effect, a family. I had heard of such things happening, of course, but this was the first time I had actually witnessed it with my own eyes.

And all sorts of beautiful things were happening: two women from Germany met at one of these dinners, discovered that they had previously been to the same charismatic church in Germany and had friends in common, and became fast friends themselves. A daughter who had left home and would not speak to, or have anything to do with, her parents received such love in one of the family dinner groups that she asked her parents' forgiveness, and moved back home. At another of the family dinners a young married woman, who was dying to get one of the new frizzy-haired permanents, had absolutely no money to spare. The permanent was a silly thing to want, she thought, but she mentioned it one Wednesday in her group. The next week some people in her group simply chipped in and gave her the money for the permanent.

And an unforeseen benefit was also emerging: the family dinners were turning out to be extremely effective evangelism tools. People began inviting their neighbors to join them, and the neighbors, who might never have accepted an invitation to a charismatic service, came. And then, touched by the Christian love and concern that they witnessed there, more than a few of them were led to the Lord, and became members of our church.

After a couple of months, the families in the groups were growing so close that they began to regret that they were not getting to know the rest of the church members as well. And so, we had, for all intents and purposes, what a square-dance caller would call "a grand right and left." The original families in each group agreed to meet together only once a month, and in the meantime they would form new groups for their weekly pot-luck get-togethers. It finally got to the point where there were as many as twenty such groups meeting on a regular basis, and our church body was being united as it had never been before.

Still another fruit of these groups was the emergence of several gifted Bible teachers, some who went on to become deacons and elders. These grew in number until we determined that Wednesday night would be Bible study night, and we would have several Bible studies in different homes. The elders would check out each new Bible study, to make sure there wasn't any conflicting teaching, and so we were able to feed our flock with the Word.

There were seven elders in Praise Center—five of them being the five directors who had made the decision to leave North County; the other two, God raised up from among the membership. If we had learned one thing as leaders in our previous situation, it was the absolute necessity of being open and honest with one another, in all of our dealings, in conference and out. More than a few of our problems had originated when one or all of us had not spoken out when we had gotten a nudge to do so, for fear of hurting someone's feelings, or being the only negative voice, or appearing foolish or just wrong. Instead, we had remained silent, and a proposal or decision which God did not want to have passed was passed. Later, we would have our consciences to face, and we would see how much better it would have been, if only we would have been willing to step on someone's toes or risk being a fool for Christ.

In fact, it had happened so often that now the elders bent over backwards to be absolutely certain that they had the leading of the Holy Spirit. They spoke every nudge and check they got, and if just one elder felt uneasy about moving forward in a given direction, they would all stop short and would not proceed further, until all were in harmony. And the extraordinary thing was that, now that the elders *were* speaking up, no one was getting offended! Everyone felt that it was so important that they move in God's will that personal feelings simply could not be allowed to be a stumbling block!

To be sure, there were a few unsettled periods in the beginning, before the final make-up of the eldership was established. But once we had the team that God had intended, the growth and deepening of Praise Center was steady and remarkable, and the interaction of the eldership today is one of the ways in which we, as a body, are praising God in our lives.

Under the elders, and being trained by them, are thirty-two men functioning in the capacity of deacons. Each of these men is given a specific area of responsibility within the body—education, music, communications, counseling, Junior Church, evangelistic outreach. Each reports monthly to an elder, with no more than five or six deacons reporting to any one elder. That may seem like a pretty structured system, especially in comparison with what had been the case at North County, but we have learned how vitally important it is that the leadership be in touch with everything that is happening. And it has been rewarding to see how quickly these men have been gaining maturity in the responsibility that we've given them.

Everywhere I looked, I began to see more instances of real caring taking place between our people. At one of the first park meetings, people who had gardens or fruit trees on their property spontaneously brought baskets of produce for other families who might be in need. And there was no embarrassment, as all were free to help themselves, because we really were a family. Similarly, a maximum effort was made to find work for any man in the congregation who was out of a job. Nobody suggested it; it just happened. But it reminded me of that fourth chapter of Acts, where the early church brought the things they had and shared them, so that none went unclothed or unfed.

A deep taproot of love was going down and was being strengthened by the adversity of not having a building of our own, or having the funds to buy land and build one. God knew what He was doing. He was building a church His way with His priorities. And as we have moved from one place to another, we have come to see just how much a church is not buildings but people. Our people know that we have been called together by God to be a church, and in everything that happens to us, collectively and individually, there is God's love and preparation.

Just how important that preparation is, no one can say. I have no idea what the future holds in store for the body of Christ on this earth, but it may well be that there will be rockslides ahead in our path. We will need strong churches then, and I would like to think that because of the work now being done, ours will be one of the strong ones. And that when heavy tribulation comes and people have to choose, our people will stand fast together.

Our walk in the wilderness, then, has been a continuing adventure, and each of us has a sense of expectation. What does God have waiting for us around the corner? For me, perhaps the most remarkable thing that happened in those formative months was how God worked out the seemingly irreconcilable dilemma of the two calls on my life.

CHAPTER • FOUR

God's Solution

Have you ever noticed how often it is the wife who first hears an alarm bell in her spirit that says something has gotten out of spiritual balance in her family? Women seem to have an intuitive gift for this. A man can become so involved with his responsibilities as provider, or with the demands and obligations on his life, that he will lose his perspective and, with it, his sensitivity to subtle shifts in the spiritual state of things, especially his own. "Honey," his wife will say, "I don't know where the next car payment is coming from either, but I think we're supposed to trust the Lord for it."

"Great!" too often comes the sarcastic reply. "I just hope He remembers it's due next Tuesday!"

Of course, wives are not immune to life's pressures—"That's fine for you to say, and I suppose Jesus is going to set the table and get dinner ready by six o'clock!"—but still, it is more often the wife who first picks up on the feeling that all is not well spiritually, with one or more of her family. This is certainly true in our family. Almost as soon as Praise Center was born, and long before I was conscious of it, Mary became aware of a growing conflict in my life: I was becoming so engrossed in the founding of our new church and making sure that it was established on solid rock, that I was seriously neglecting the national ministry, which was still the primary call of God upon my life. What's more, as Praise Center continued to grow, she foresaw that I would become so totally involved that the national ministry could almost cease to be functional.

From time to time, she would try to point this out to me, and whenever she did, it frustrated me, because I saw no other alternative to my present course of action. I knew that God had also called me to be His instrument in raising up a church in Southern California, and I was determined not to repeat the mistakes I had made at North County. I was not going to be a figurehead pastor. God was holding me responsible for Praise Center, and this time I was determined that I would prove worthy of His trust.

But Mary loved me so much that she was willing to persevere with me to get me back in the right place. And when she was finally able to make me hear what she was saying, I could see the truth in it. Indeed, I had been aware of it when we left North County. When Praise Center first came into being, the Lord made it clear to us and the directors that it was to be subordinate to the foundation—an active support to the foundation's world-wide outreach, and a living testament of what can happen when a group of people really commit themselves to putting praise to work in our individual and corporate lives. Right from the start, anyone considering membership in Praise Center was given to understand the center's primary missionary outreach was the work that the foundation was doing, and that with all the prisons and foreign countries that were opening up, there was more work than they could possibly handle.

Nevertheless, I had become so involved in building up the church and, this time, keeping in close touch with everything that was happening, that before long my workday was spent 75 percent on the center and 25 percent on the foundation, when it should have been the other way around. And the worst of it was, even after I saw the truth of what Mary said, and the danger of it, I couldn't see how I could change what I was doing.

Mary could, though; for years she had been praying that God would send a full-time pastor to help me and free me to be doing the things He had first called me to. Now, more than ever, that right-hand man was needed, and especially, Mary prayed, one who had a gift for all the organizational and administrative details that were so time-consuming. But nowhere on the horizon did such a man appear.

And then finally, God nearly had to hit me over the head. *His* man for the job was and had been there all the time, right under our noses!

It happened at about two o'clock on a very hot afternoon, when I was over at the little house which we were renting to use as office space for the foundation and the center. The place was a bit frantic, as always. Velma Beck was manning the phone, which was almost constantly ringing; my daughter, Joann, was handling—or rather, trying to handle—the incoming mail; Carol and Cherry were typing correspondence; in an unused corner, Dean was putting together the foundation's monthly newsletter; and Marilyn Wyman was trying to give the whole place some semblance of organization. And then, on top of our regulars, every spare inch of space was filled with volunteers. Things were so crowded and busy that I had long ago relinquished the room that was to be my office, and now, when I wanted to have a private conversation with someone, we would resort to a pair of old lawn chairs under a big shade tree in the backyard.

Personally, I really preferred this open-air office, with the peace of the wind rustling the leaves overhead, and perhaps a tall glass of iced tea in my hand. And that afternoon, in the other chair sat Roy Wyman, one of the associate pastors who had come with us from North County. Roy had also been my administrative assistant there, and a more loyal friend and support throughout the trouble could not be found. Such was our relationship that I could confide in him and count on the honesty of his response; he would speak for the Holy Spirit, even if I didn't necessarily want to hear what he had to say.

Roy was four years older than I was, an extremely successful businessman who at one time owned four beauty colleges, where women came to learn how to be beauticians. In addition he also ran six beauty salons. But when he joined our staff at North County, he had simply sold his businesses and retired to be able to devote all his energy and concentration to performing whatever tasks God would lay before him. Roy had more genuine Christian concern for others than any man I knew. I held his counsel in high esteem, and was eager to seek it now.

"Roy," I said, deciding to lay it right on the line. "I cannot go on being Praise Center's full-time pastor or having the people think I am. The foundation has not been getting the attention it deserves, and I have a feeling that God is about to lift His grace, if I don't start doing what I am supposed to be doing. Somebody else is going to have to take over the main pastoring responsibility—and soon, because our people cannot be permitted to go on thinking of me as their main pastor. It's not fair to them and it's hurting the foundation." I paused, and then plunged ahead. "Roy, God is telling me that you are to be the pastor in charge of Praise Center." I had to take a deep breath then, for I knew that Roy did not want to be in charge of anything. "I know you don't feel that you are prepared to take on such a responsibility but God has called you and He doesn't make mistakes."

Noticing the big smile on Roy's face I stopped; amusement was the last response I expected.

"Merlin, this is really hard to believe," he exclaimed, and broke into a hearty chuckle. "God is really something! I had something I wanted to talk to *you* about today; in fact, it was something I've been meaning to talk to you about for some time, and today I'd finally gotten my courage up. And then the Lord makes it so easy!" He shook his head in wonder, and I furrowed my brow in perplexity; what *was* he talking about?

"Here it is," he went on, taking a deep breath. "Recently the Lord has been impressing on me that He wants me to accept the responsibilities for Praise Center." He smiled. "And I had resisted the impression, not because I questioned the call, but because I am aware of my total lack of qualifications to fill such a post. But now. . . ."

It was my turn to smile, for my heart was already signaling the confirmation jubilantly. I was only surprised that something so obviously the Lord had completely escaped my notice for so long.

"It's the Lord, all right," I said, reaching over and putting my hand on his shoulder, "and we'll seek His timing as to when the formal ordination should be. I'm absolutely sure God has called you and anointed you to be our pastor."

That night after supper, I told Mary the news. She laughed. "I always felt it would be someone with special administrative abilities, but I can see that above all, Roy's gift of love for others is what qualifies him in God's eyes."

I nodded. "He has a true pastor's heart," I said, "and Praise Center needs that, far more than anything else."

We did not make the announcement right away, but it pleased me to see how many people seemed to be picking it up in their spirits, and turning more and more to Roy for counseling. And on his part, Roy was becoming more and more involved in their lives. Sometimes, when God gives us advance notice of a change He will be making in our circumstances, we anticipate Him, and in our enthusiasm actually mess things up. Real wisdom dictates that we praise and thank Him for it, and then just wait patiently until He brings it to pass.

Roy was ordained as pastor of Praise Center on June 19, 1977, with our singing group, The Joyful Praise, providing music the Holy Spirit had given specially for this occasion. I was so grateful and so full of joy, that when it came time for me to explain to the congregation the significance of what we were about to do, I couldn't speak. Tears of joy flowed down my cheeks and hopefully said all that needed to be said.

Later, Roy's wife, Marilyn, told Mary that Roy had always known I loved him in the Lord, but until that moment he had not realized how much.

With Roy installed as pastor, and me kicked upstairs, as it were, to be "minister-at-large," I felt as if a ponderous burden had been lifted from my shoulders. I still preached three Sundays a month and met with Roy and the elders from time to time, but it was completely different now; the running of the church was in Roy's hands, and at last I was free to concentrate on the foundation.

Under Roy's leadership, things have gone as smoothly as one could possibly hope for. And new and exciting innovations are happening all the time. For instance, intercessory prayer has now become a significant part of the center's outreach. In addition to our prayer line (714-743-LIFE) on which we receive prayer and counseling requests from everywhere, we have a prayer chain that goes into action the moment an urgent request is received, with one person calling another and alerting them to the need. We have had some remarkable answers to prayer, but the main blessing to us has been the spirit in our church which has come from serious and sustained prayer for others. On a level that I don't fully understand, it is deepening our awareness and sensitivity to the needs of others in *all* aspects of our daily lives, and making us a little less self-oriented in our daily walk.

And membership in Praise Center has become something very meaningful to our people. Where once it had been simply a matter of attending church regularly, now there was a formal course of instruction, covering all elements of being a Christian—salvation, baptism, baptism in the Holy

Spirit, the gifts of the Holy Spirit, home, marriage, personal relationships, and so on. A strong emphasis is placed on our commitment to one another, as well as to God, and everyone who is able to tithe is encouraged to do so.

Another thing that is stressed is that members are undertaking a responsibility to pray for their pastors—and that now includes another member of our pastorate, Vic Stout. Vic is a big, blond broad-shouldered lad who came out of the drug culture and whose huge six-foot-six-inch frame and love of fishing bring to mind Peter, the fisherman who Jesus called to be a "fisher of men." How ironic that the Lord would transform a violent and rebellious nature into a spirit that radiates the gentleness and peace of Jesus.

So many other good things have happened to Praise Center that it would be impossible to list them all. However, the outstanding aspect of Praise Center was summed up in the words of one visitor: "When I stepped inside, something came over me. I looked around trying to decide why this church was affecting me so strongly. And then I realized that these people loved one another. The longer I stayed, the more I realized that they loved me too."

CHAPTER • FIVE

The Public Eye

God has a sense of humor, and sometimes He uses it to sharpen our own, particularly when we begin to take ourselves a mite too seriously. A perfect example of His giving us an intimation of what He one day intends to do with us and our anticipating His timetable a bit prematurely, is what happened with the whole business of television.

One morning, about a year before we left North County, the Lord made it clear to me that He intended to use television as an instrument to spread the message of praise. And I got excited! The major Christian networks reached millions of people, and now, with the satellite projects they were working on, they would one day have 24-hour-a-day broadcasting to the entire world! Imagine people in Africa and South America learning that praise could change their lives! People who might never have an opportunity to read the praise books could be reached electronically.

When I got home, I was so enthusiastic, I could

hardly wait to share the news with Mary. But to my surprise, what had seemed to me like a dream about to come true struck her as a nightmare. "That's fine for you, Merlin, and I'm happy for you," she said. "But I know what's going to happen: you're going to want me with you, and if there's one thing I don't want to do, it's go on television!" The Lord gave me the wisdom to keep my mouth shut, and she relented. "But whatever God wants," she said, smiling gamely.

Far from being discouraged, I started making phone calls to anyone who knew anyone in television, and I began to get a picture of what was actually involved in producing and distributing television shows. The main thing I learned was that it was prohibitively expensive. To make a one-half-hour show the way it should be done, with topflight professionals and first-class equipment, would cost well in excess of a thousand dollars, and would mean going up to Los Angeles, a grueling two-hour drive. And then, to get anything approaching national distribution would be even more expensive. Looking at it from the practical side, it was really more than the foundation could afford at the time.

So I proceeded to see if there weren't some less expensive way of accomplishing that goal. And of course, there was. I located a local cable TV station in San Diego. They weren't NBC, but I thought they were a good place to begin.

I'll never forget the night Mary and I were going

back to Escondido after one particularly disastrous taping session. Mary was upset. "If you could have seen that big potted plant creeping across the stage behind you, you would have broken up!"

The memory of just how ludicrous the whole thing had appeared did just that for Mary, and she broke into gales of laughter. It was a minute before she could go on.

"And then there was that second cameraman, apparently inspired to 'artistic heights' by getting a truly original camera angle. It was original all right:a close-up of the back of your head! I mean, really! Who wants to see the back of your head!"

I laughed and tried to concentrate on the road, and laughed again. And Mary continued to enlighten me. "He must have been really proud of that shot, and the director must have been anxious to encourage him, because he held it . . . and held it, and held it. 'Okay,' I thought, 'we've seen the back of his head and his bald spot, now how about moving on to something else?' But the camera stayed right there; this was going to be a landmark in innovative television!" Once again Mary broke into laughter, in spite of herself.

"Well," she laughed, "you know how I'm not good at hiding my feelings when I get upset." I nodded, finding it hard to keep a straight face, as she continued. "Well, I finally tried to get the director's attention to get him to shift the camera to something else. And you know what? I really think he saw me, though he acted as if he hadn't. But when the show was over, it was pretty obvious how I felt about things." And now I was laughing as hard as she was. "You know what I overheard him say? 'Merlin's wife sure has a lot to learn about praising the Lord.' And he's not even a charismatic!" With that, we both convulsed with laughter.

With this unforgettable introduction, or should I say initiation, into the exciting and sometimes unpredictable world of television, I pressed on, overcoming one obstacle after another. Finally, our perseverance was rewarded and we had our first half-hour program in the can, ready to be broadcast.

How was it? Mary's reaction the night we watched that first program, to which we'd given our all, spoke volumes in a few well-chosen words: "Merlin, it's so hokey, it's embarrassing!"

And she was right, of course. The lighting was . . .shall we say, peculiar. There was usually only one camera operating, so we were looking straight at the lens. Apparently the cameraman was not too familiar with the zoom lens, for it seemed to take off in the most unexpected directions. All of a sudden, there would be a close-up of my lip, or some other feature, larger than life, foisted upon our viewing audience through the wonders of twentieth-century technology! At times he would forget the parameters of the set, and mike booms or other equipment would suddenly loom into view. And from time to time, someone would stroll right in front of the camera, in the middle of the show!

And yet all these quirks and flaws proved to be a blessing in disguise, because they served to distract attention from my own performance, which was so wooden it may have called to mind that well-known figure from the pages of our past, in feathered headdress, perpetually on duty in front of many a cigar store.

Spontaneity was not to be left to chance. So concerned had I been that I not fluff my presentation, that I had practically memorized it, and that's just exactly how it came across. I was also acutely aware that our friends would be among the thousands of people (hopefully) who would be watching. As a result, with time, this self-consciousness increased, and particularly after the reactions—or rather, nonreactions—of some of our friends. They never so much as mentioned the program, and if the subject did come up in their presence, they would sort of smile and say nothing.

Was I disheartened? Did it dawn on me that perhaps it was not yet God's time? Not on your life! Obviously what was needed was more expertise!

Next, I tried to locate an even less expensive way to get into television. And there was one: we could borrow the equipment of a local junior college and do the shows with college instructors. This *seemed* ideal. Professional equipment and professional instructors! What more could one ask for? But this proved to be an even greater disaster in Merlin

Carothers' television career.

Need I say more?

In looking back we came to appreciate God's wonderful sense of humor in the whole thing. We were obviously ahead of His timetable; nevertheless, He made good use of it, giving us experience that would prove invaluable for the future.

Then came the troubles at North County, and I was sure that would be the end of television for us. I was no longer concerned that anyone who knew us, or was even familiar with our ministry, would pay any attention to what was being said about us. But TV networks had to be extremely careful, and I doubted that we would have anything further to do in television, for a long, long time to come.

There's an old World Series saying: Never bet against the Yankees. There's an even older saying having to do with a Christian predicting his future: Never say never. Never say that there is one thing that categorically will *not* happen, because God just might surprise you. In the spring of 1977, I received a call from a successful advertising executive, Dick Myers, who was newly Spirit-filled and who felt God had told him we were to make a series of television shows.

"That's very interesting," I said, as kindly as I could, "and when the Lord tells me the same thing, I'd love to get together with you and talk about it." But he was persistent and persuasive. Finally, what he had in mind began to make sense: thirteen one-hour programs, complete with music by some of the top Christian entertainers in the country, and including interviews with the best-known Christian leaders and authors on the subject of praise. There would even be Christian puppets! Something to draw the interest of every member of the family. Wouldn't I at least pray about it?

How can anyone say no to that kind of a request? So I prayed, but having been burned rather badly in the not too distant past and being a bit "gun-shy" after the whole North County business, I was so skeptical that it would have taken a miracle to change my heart. Yet that was exactly what happened. I seemed to be getting a clear indication from the Lord to go ahead. Not trusting my own discernment, I asked Mary as well as Roy and Marilyn to pray, too. They got the same leading. So, much to my surprise, I found myself on a plane to New Jersey to meet with Dick Myers, who was eminently qualified to put together a quality TV program.

He was delighted! The production would take place in the studio of a major network and would employ some of the very top men in the profession. And the fact that the men, the equipment and the studio were all coincidentally available, all at the same time, was one more indication that God's time was now!

I could soon see why my new friend was such a success. After several more weeks of preparations, I made the first of two taping trips to Philadelphia.

In the beginning, everything that could go wrong went wrong. They were weird things, like overhead spotlights beginning to blow, one after another, as if someone were deliberately popping them out in a shooting gallery. A cameraman who had worked the lights for twelve years told me that this was impossible! But there was no denying the reality of this impossibility.

I was faced with two possibilities: either I had run ahead of the Lord again, which was the one thing I least wanted to do, or Satan was kicking up a storm over the prospect of some really good programs carrying the praise message to millions. After listening carefully in my spirit, I felt I could rule out the former. We really had prayed as earnestly as we knew how, to make sure we weren't second-guessing God again, and we had received nothing but encouragement from Him, since the decision to proceed. No, this was a case of the "Old Boy" having himself a field day! He was putting on a special "light show" to keep us in the dark.

There are two ways to deal with the devil, when he is kicking up a fuss. We can expend a great deal of time and energy, rebuking him and banishing him and expelling this demon and that evil spirit. Or we can simply fill the room with praise to God in the highest. Instead of giving the devil far more than his due, and possibly inducing fear in those around us with less understanding, doesn't it make more sense to elevate Jesus, and make *Him* the center of our attention? It has been my experience that, just as our praise is a sweet-smelling savor in God's nostrils, it is the exact opposite in Satan's, and a very effective demonic "insect-repellent."

I praised God for every wire that suddenly started to smoke and every light that inexplicably burst. The more that happened, the more I praised the Lord, quietly but deeply; and gaining enthusiasm with each incident, I was literally chuckling for joy. And all of a sudden, harassment ceased, as discord and chaos were replaced by a beautiful presence of the Lord. I wanted to shout "Hallelujah!" or "Jesus is Lord!" and some other appropriate things, but I just stood there, silently beaming and thanking God in my heart. Silence seemed to be appropriate, for God was demonstrating the reality of "Be still and know that I am God."

The whole episode had quite an effect on the technicians and directors; several of them expressed awe at my composure. At the height of our most exasperating difficulties, one came up and said, "I'm telling you, if this was happening to any of the other emcees whom we've done programing for, they would have blown their tops by now!" That gave me an opportunity to do a little witnessing for the Lord, and soon the remainder of the production proceeded with professional smoothness. An unseen hand seemed to operate behind the scenes and order reigned, even as chaos had before. Praise cleared the atmosphere.

The series was a success beyond our greatest expectations (though our friends confided that the puppets stole the show), and a major network vice-president commented that it was the best Christian programing he had seen. Best of all, a number of the studio people made a point of coming up afterwards and saying that while their minds had previously been completely closed to any Christian message, they were open now. Up to the present, these programs have been seen by millions of people in over fifty-five cities and broadcast over one satellite network.

Back home in Escondido, a couple of months later, in July, I was taking a rare afternoon off, having just gotten home from a two-day crusade. I had just dozed off on our patio when the phone rang. It was the programing director of the Trinity Broadcasting Network in Los Angeles. They had a proposal to make concerning the possibility of my doing some work for them. We made an appointment.

TBN is a rapidly growing Christian network. At the time I went to see them, they had only one station, but their growth has been phenomenal, to say the least. As of this writing, a little more than a year later, they now own, or are negotiating to buy, twelve more stations, in addition to being carried on twenty-six full-broadcast stations and more than 300 cable TV stations.

From the moment I walked into their studio, I had

a good feeling—God was there, and He was using that place. And in the programing director's office, he did me the kindness of leveling with me right off the bat. "Before I tell you what we have in mind," he said, "would you mind telling me, in your own words, what exactly happened down there with North County Christian Center? I have to ask, because we've heard some pretty wild stuff, and I'd like to hear your version. Do you mind?"

I sighed, "No, I don't mind." But actually, I did. I was sick and tired of having to drag through the whole mess yet another time. Why couldn't people just let it rest? But I felt the Lord's grace then, and silently prayed to recall the things that needed to be said.

Sensing my hesitance, the programing director was apologetic. "I'm really sorry to have to put you through this, Merlin, but it's necessary. Through our ministry here, TBN has featured a number of Christian pastors and authors and helped them to become nationally known. And in a couple of cases, after they gained national prominence, something really awful would surface out of their past or present, and it really gave the network a black eye, because we had been instrumental in promoting them. It's been more than a little disillusioning, and we're making sure it won't happen again. For instance, we've already had a couple of our people check pretty extensively into the North County thing, and now I need to hear it from you."

I nodded and proceeded to tell him all the details—far more than I have outlined in the first two chapters of this book. When I finished, he thanked me and said, "That concurs item for item with what we had learned on our own." He stood up. "Good! We'll be having a board of directors meeting shortly, and we will be praying about doing a daily program with you. If we get the Lord's go-ahead, it will mean a sixty-five-program series, half an hour a day. . . ."

"Sixty-five programs?" I interrupted him.

"That's right," he looked at me, surprised at my surprise. "Five days a week for thirteen weeks," he went on in his matter-of-fact way. "We will assume all production and distribution expenses, and it will be first-class all the way. But it's going to require a great deal of your time. We would like to tape a week's worth of shows in two days, possibly even one when we get the routine down. So you will need to pray about it, too, and see if you're prepared to make that kind of commitment. Because once we start, we're going to have to go straight on through."

A little dazed at the rapidly developing prospects, I thanked him and started down I-5 to Escondido. *Father in heaven*, I thought, *you really are something! Here, I knock myself out, trying everything I can possibly think of to get started in television, and then you, in the twinkling of an eye, set the whole thing in motion. When am I going to learn to have the patience to wait on you?*

A week later, when TBN called, I was happy to

agree. And so began an extremely demanding, but exciting adventure. On many of the shows, Mary, reluctantly, appeared with me. I was glad to have her companionship, and, I must selfishly add, her help with the driving, because often I didn't have five messages prepared by the time I was due to leave for the studio. But despite all of the pressure, there was such exceptional grace covering the taping sessions, that once we were actually taping, everything went unbelievably smooth. We rarely had to back up and re-tape a segment, and I seemed to be remarkably at peace inside, even when my voice would begin to give out in the middle of the fifth program in a row.

God's blessing in the studio was somehow transferred onto the tape, as well. When they started airing the show at the beginning of fall '77, it drew the greatest viewer response of any show they had done. What's more, it kept building, so that when we had taped the last of the sixty-five shows, they asked me if I couldn't please do forty more. Another eight weeks! We prayed, and the answer came, *Go ahead.* I agreed. The second series went as well as the first, and were as well received. After the forty, they wanted me to do still another series, but by that time I could hear the Lord telling me to take a break.

The effect of the TV series on the foundation's outreach was incalculable. As part of TBN's own ministry, they bought a large quantity of our books and offered them over the air—free—to anyone who wrote in requesting them. And each time they sent out a book, they would share the address with us, so that our mailing list started growing rapidly and ultimately more than tripled. With TBN's entry into satellite broadcasting, each program started going out three times during the day and three times during the night, so that any station in America which wanted it could broadcast it. Thousands of viewing Christians who had never met us now began to think of us almost as part of their families. "Oh, Merlin and Mary," a little lady whom we had never met would say to us in some distant state, "I just wanted you to know that I have breakfast with you every morning!"

But the Lord had one more television surprise in store for me. Last fall I was invited to be on Jim Bakker's "PTL Club." And while we were on the air, Jim said that the Lord had just impressed him that he was to offer *Prison to Praise* to anyone who wrote in and requested a copy. And then he told of his own personal experience with this book.

In his early days, before he had started his own program, he was going through one of his deepest struggles, when he happened to read *Prison to Praise*. It so changed his outlook, that he began praising God in the midst of his problems, and the moment he did, God began giving him new vision and insight.

Jim closed the program that day by attributing the formation of the vast PTL network to his initially learning to praise God. And then he offered the book.

When we went off the air, he turned to me and said, "Well, Merlin, we may need 50,000 books."

They wound up needing 110,000.

After the PTL program, the foundation began receiving calls from TV stations all over the country, asking us if we had any shows on tape that they might air (at no expense to us), and we were able to send them prints of the TBN series. Also, PTL requested the Philadelphia series for their satellite, and as a result of these and other developments, our shows are now being seen in more than 170 cities!

And God was doing it all—without me trying to pull any strings whatsoever. That was the lesson that He had been trying to get through to me, throughout the entire TV episode: I didn't have to *push*. If God was in it, He would open the doors. And I was to *follow*, not run ahead.

But it's not always easy, when you have an overwhelming desire to accomplish something for Him. In my natural self, I still wanted to get all the wagons lined up behind me—the foundation, Praise Center, the prison ministry, the TV and the books—and then pull them.

It is almost incomprehensible how quickly and completely I could forget the lesson that had just been so lovingly taught. But that is what happened. And it started with a computer—not a huge, grandiose IBM, but it might as well have been for all the grandiose headaches and frustrations it programed into our lives!

CHAPTER • SIX

The Perfect Answer

Along with the foundation's sudden, rapid growth came a whole new set of problems; indeed, as our mailing list doubled and was on the verge of redoubling, our required correspondence now seemed to expand geometrically. And it was getting more complex. People were now inquiring about coordinating crusades with video programming, obtaining a speaker as well as books for a prison ministry, and about the possibility of their sponsoring the programs on their own local cable stations. And now, many prisoners were writing in, praising God for the books, and asking if there wasn't someone they might correspond with.

Every one of these letters deserved a thoughtful, prayerful reply, and they were in addition to the hundreds of letters a week that we had been receiving regularly from old friends sending prayer requests, praise reports and gifts, and new ones jubilantly praising God and requesting my prayers for an urgent concern. All of these, too, needed to be answered, and by the fall of '77, we had increased our staff to fifteen, and had moved to larger quarters in a one-story business building in downtown Escondido.

But even with the increase, our correspondence department was unable to cope with the mounting demands put upon it. Our responses began to be late getting out, and their accuracy was slipping. Even worse, our burgeoning mailing list was beginning to get confused. It became increasingly clear to all of us that a major improvement would have to be made, and soon.

About this time, a new Christian, with extensive experience in advertising and promotion, joined our staff. With great enthusiasm he helped us to look into the future and plan for it, so that the problems we were now facing would not become insurmountable before we could prepare for them. With my blessing, he began extensive research into how to best cope with our multifaceted and speedily growing problems. After a number of weeks, he recommended that we buy a computer—specifically one with the newest, most sophisticated, mini-computers yet designed, a model that had just appeared on the market and was touted as being the perfect answer for small but rapidly growing organizations such as our own. This machine would keep all the incoming information straight; organize our mailing list and from it give us more correct information than we could ever imagine; keep track of all our records and accounts; address our monthly newsletter; watch our inventory of books and alert us when we needed to order more; do our staff payroll; and much more besides. About the only thing it didn't do was vacuum the office carpeting, but we suspected that a later modification would soon rectify this oversight!

It had only one drawback: it was astronomically expensive. It would cost far more than the foundation had in available funds, and we were very much against the foundation's ever going into debt. Up to this point, God had always provided the money we needed, when we needed it, although sometimes He seemed to wait until the eleventh hour to do so. It kept us trusting and relying on Him totally, and we were loathe to do anything that would violate that pattern. So all of us on the staff spent much time in prayer, seeking direction.

While we were trying to decide, something happened which made the necessity for taking some positive action even more urgent. Up to now, we had been renting time on the computer of a large local business, servicing our mailing list and addressing our newsletter by means of a time-sharing arrangement. But now that business informed us that they really needed the time on the computer themselves, and would we please make other arrangements.

So after going over and over the situation, we finally made the decision that we thought God was leading us to, and I went ahead and ordered the computer. We had enough money to make the down payment, and would have to pay the remainder in monthly installments. The computer needed to be in an air-conditioned room, so my office was sacrificed to this electronic wonder, and soon it was installed. With its gleaming metallic surfaces and its imposing control panel and impressive video display screen, it held us all in awe.

There was only one minor problem: it was so new that it was not quite operational. Nothing to be concerned about, the company assured us; they were working on a final modification which would have it operational in thirty days, and they positively guaranteed that it would be fulfilling all its functions within sixty days. That seemed reasonable, and so we informed the business with whom we had the time-sharing agreement that we had made other arrangements and wouldn't be needing their services.

But sixty days became ninety days, and whenever we called the computer company to beg them to send a field engineer to work on it, they assured us that someone would "soon" be there. But when ninety days had become six months, and the thing still wasn't working right, our situation was desperate. The business whose computer we had been time-sharing, finally reached the end of their patience with us and informed us that we simply could not go on having "just one more month." And we finally reached the end of our patience with the computer company. Under pressure, they guaranteed that they would at least have the computer ready to run off a set of labels for our newsletter, in time for the next issue to get out on schedule.

And they did. It was only later that we discovered that this mighty electronic wizard had somehow managed to incorporate into our list all the names that had previously been deleted, plus all the addresses, old and new, which had been corrected. In addition, it had inexplicably ignored many of our regular recipients, with the result that some people got four newsletters, while others got none at all. It was as if someone had taken one of those old card-shuffling machines and deliberately shuffled our list! Many addresses have still not been recovered.

Anyone who has ever dealt with a mailing list of any size probably is familiar with the headache that came next. The entire list would now have to be sorted out by hand—a prodigious task under the best of circumstances, when you had a dozen people who could spend full-time on it. As it was, we had two people whom we really couldn't spare, and we had to ask for volunteers. And on top of everything else, for this gleaming, bleeping electronic millstone, in a very short time we would have to pay a prodigious amount which we did not have.

There was only one solution: I would have to accept

more speaking engagements and try to raise the necessary money.

"But, Lord," I cried, *"how?"* In those days, I was preaching nearly every Sunday, and so most of Sunday was spent at the Praise Center services, preaching and praying and ministering and fellowshiping. I looked forward to Sundays all week and enjoyed meeting friends old and new. But the fellowshiping could also be tremendously draining. Sunday was definitely not a day of rest.

Monday, I would wake up, and the first thing on my mind would be to start right in working on next Sunday's sermon, because the way my weeks were going, it had to be right away, or never. The sermon weighed heavily on my mind. There would be visitors from all over the country, expecting to hear a special word. And the people of Praise Center—they, too, undoubtedly hoped to hear something fresh and glowing from their preacher. So, the first thing after breakfast, I would head back upstairs to my study, to prepare a sermon outline.

But no sooner am I at my desk, than an even more pressing need comes to mind: I have to have five television sermons ready by tomorrow morning! In desperation, I yank open my sermon file drawer and start thumbing through old sermons, then pull out my Bible and start thumbing through it, crying out, "Lord, I need five anointed messages right away!" But of course, nothing comes until I give up my anxiety, and accept His peace and start praising Him for the gift of the television series, for the fact that I haven't the foggiest notion of what I am going to talk about, for the fact that no matter how hopeless the situation seems, He is still very much in charge.

And gradually, as I praise, I quiet down inside. And as I do, I begin to hear that still, small voice.

I have three TV sermons outlined and am starting on the fourth, when the phone rings. It's Dean Nygaard, the editor of our newsletter as well as the center's lead musician. "Merlin, sorry to bother you, but I'm afraid we need you down here. We just got a call that this month's newsletter will not go out on time if we don't get it over to them within the hour, and you still haven't given it your final approval."

"Well, how come it wasn't ready sooner?" I snapped.

"Uh, the printer said that the typesetting was delayed because Reverend Carothers did not get his article finished in time."

Gulp. "I'm sorry, Dean. It will be ready on time next month."

"Uh, Merlin? Do you suppose that you might ever be able to get *two* months ahead? And Mary, too? It would sure make a difference."

I agree and head for the office, but privately I don't hold out much hope. I go over the newsletter which looks fine, and begin to tackle some of the work which has piled up on my desk, asking someone to get me a sandwich for lunch, because I'm anxious to get back to my study and complete the two remaining sermons for tomorrow.

Just then Roy's voice comes over the intercom: "Merlin, can you come to the hospital with me, to pray for Janet Foray's mother? They don't expect her to live out the day."

"Well, I—of course."

When we've finished praying, I take my leave of Roy and slip out, only to be cornered in the corridor by an acquaintance who simply *has* to talk right then and there. It will only take him a minute, he assures me, but it takes more like half an hour. By the time I get home, my mind is so frazzled that it's impossible to concentrate on the remaining TV sermons. So for a change of pace, I shift over to the topic of next Sunday's sermon. But of course I can't hear the Holy Spirit any more clearly on that subject than on the former. There I am, waiting for the Lord to give me inspiration and mentally drumming my fingers on the desk. Of course, nothing comes, and I stare out the window in consternation.

Then Mary's voice comes up the stairway: "Merlin? Dinner's ready." *Dinner?* Already? With mounting frustration, I go downstairs and attempt to put my concerns aside and concentrate on what happened to Mary and Bruce and Genie during their day. As soon as dinner is over, however, I go physically back upstairs to where I was mentally all the time.

But now, for some reason, I notice what I had somehow overlooked all day long: a stack of mail for my immediate attention that is at least six inches high. And on top is a note from our crusade secretary pleading with me to please take care of these, and some of the speaking requests have been waiting two or three weeks for a reply. Chagrined, I start to work on the pile, and in a couple of hours, have managed to answer all the most pressing correspondence.

Underneath them, however, I discover a folder of ⟵ urgent prayer requests, and I read each and hold it up to the Lord, asking Him to take a hand in the situation, and believing that He has already begun to do so. Beneath that folder is yet another, this one containing prayer requests that have come in via our prayer lines. These, too, I raise to the Father's throne with a sense of joy, knowing that we have a corps of dedicated volunteers who are already praying for all of these spiritual needs.

By the time I finish, it's late, and all I want to do is get to bed. But then I remember that one of the staff reminded me that I would have to let her know tomorrow how many requests from prison chaplains we will be able to honor with free books. And so, I go through that folder, deciding how many books we can afford to send where, and finally join Mary who's been reading in the bedroom.

Tuesday morning I get up an hour early, to see if I can't at least get one more TV sermon ready, before we leave for Los Angeles. I thank God that Mary is going with me for this trip; I'll prevail upon her to drive, while I get the last one done in the car. And by the grace of God, I do have one more done by breakfast, and work on the last one in the car, finishing just as Mary turns into the studio's parking lot. As we're walking into the studio, I try to outline to Mary what I'm going to be talking about on the five shows, but I go over them so quickly, she bites her lip and says, "Praise the Lord, I'll just have to trust Him to put the right words in my mouth when I'm supposed to speak."

And of course, He does. There is a smooth flow to everything and a discernable linking of theme to theme, which can only be the Holy Spirit.

But after five hours or so, under those studio lights, where the temperature is twenty degrees hotter than it is elsewhere in the building, we have had some technical difficulties and have only gotten three shows done, which means we will have to come back later in the week. Wearily, soaking wet, we gather up the two changes of clothes we have already gone through, and head for the car. I drive, and Mary falls asleep.

When we get home, Mary hurries to start getting dinner ready, and I resolutely head back upstairs to see if I can get Sunday's sermon. I am sitting at my desk, trying to keep from dozing, when Mary calls up the stairs: "Remember, you've got to get some clothes out. You've got a crusade in Indianapolis tomorrow, and the plane leaves at nine-thirty in the morning."

Indianapolis! For the moment, I had forgotten

about it. I found a clean suit and underwear and shirts and praised God that Mary had a gift for packing. "Merlin?" It's Mary again. "Did you arrange for the tickets?"

"Tickets? Oh, Lord, I hope my faithful secretary thought to take care of them!"

A phone call reveals that she had; they are on my desk.

The next morning, I am up bright and early for the drive to the San Diego airport. Into my attache case I put all the correspondence that still needs to be answered. I am thankful for the time on the airplane, which will give me a chance to get caught up. And indeed, the plane trip is a blessing. Not only do I finish the correspondence, and begin to get the gist of a message for the crusade, but I even have time to close my eyes for a while.

At the airport I am met by two excited couples who are bubbling over with anticipation of the night ahead. In the car they share all the wonderful things that the Lord has been doing in their lives, asking questions, yet hardly pausing long enough for me to give an answer. Which is all right with me, because inwardly I am praying for the Lord to both help me to concentrate on what they are saying, and yet to also give me the rest of what He wants me to speak on.

Traffic is heavier than anticipated, so there is no time to eat; indeed, by the time we reach our destination, the meeting has already begun. They escort me up to the platform, and I can sense the expectation in the audience. "Oh, Lord, I hope they're not going to be disappointed! Jesus, help me, let it be you and not me." Before I know it, I am introduced, and I step up to the microphone. "Father, I am not prepared. Either you will provide the message by your Spirit, or I am going to stand up here and look awfully stupid."

But once again, God in His mercy anoints the meeting and supplies all that is needed. People are touched, and many come forward to accept the Lord. Then others come forward to be prayed for to receive the baptism in the Holy Spirit, and still others come forward to be prayed for, for healing. And we have a glorious time.

By the time it is finished, it is late, and I am ready to collapse. But two other excited couples come up—how can they still have so much energy?—and tell me that they have arranged an "afterglow" meeting at one of their homes. I am about to beg off, when one of them mentions that there will be food, and I recall that I haven't eaten since a snack lunch on the airplane. Futhermore, it is now so late that I won't be able to get anything at the motel where I'll be staying. So, my spirits revive. But, it turns out that there are so many people, and they have so much to share all at the same time, that, apart from some cheese and crackers that my hostess manages to get to me, there's no time to eat. Again, I have to ask the Lord to help me keep focused on what they are saying and pray coherently when asked to pray, and not to look at my watch as it gets to be twelve-thirty and then one o'clock.

Eventually, my eyes start to fall shut. Someone notices and asks if I would like to go to my motel. I would. Yet no sooner am I in bed, than I am staring wide-eyed at the ceiling, too tired to fall asleep. So, I take a hot bath, and, just as I'm beginning to relax, I remember that I have forgotten to set my alarm clock. I get up and set it for five, as my plane is scheduled to leave at six-twenty. I'm taking the early flight, because I must get home in time to get a few things done, as the next day, Thursday, we are due back in Los Angeles to finish the week's taping.

By Saturday, I am completely wrung out and still haven't had a chance to get Sunday's sermon ready. Well, thank God it's Saturday, and the foundation office is closed. I'll have the whole day at home to wait on the Lord, and see what sort of word He will give me.

"Dad," Bruce said at breakfast, "you remember that you promised to go look at an old car with me some Saturday." I nodded; I had promised—several weeks ago.

"Yes, but long before he promised you," Genie broke in, "he told *me* that he would take me horseback riding."

"Neither one of those things does he do, until he fixes the door to the clothes dryer," Mary chimes in with a laugh. "I've been waiting *months* for him to do that!"

I smile and say nothing. But inside I am frustrated—no, angry—and not at my family, but at God, because obviously my family came first, especially after I had been gone for most of the week. But when was I going to get that sermon done? And the fact that it was God who I was annoyed with only frustrated me all the more, because God was never wrong. So, through clenched teeth, I praise Him—and keep at it, until I really begin to mean it, deep in my heart.

Then I can fix the dryer with a cheerful spirit, and enjoy horseback riding with Genie and going to look at the car with Bruce. And that takes care of Saturday. But I have one ace in the hole, and after dinner, while the others are clearing dishes and washing up, I slip upstairs to my study. I have just gotten out my pad and pencil, when I hear someone arriving at the house. No problem; Mary will explain that I'm working and—

"Merlin? You'd better come down here. You've got a visitor." And then, sensing my hesitation, she adds, "She's eighteen months old and is asking for you."

Well, why didn't you say so, I think, tossing aside my pencil and hurrying downstairs. My granddaughter Andrea is a two-foot vision of loveliness, standing a little unsteadily in the middle of the living room. "Pa Pa, Pa Pa!" she calls, when she sees me, and I swoop down upon my hands and knees and gobble her up, to her shrieks of delight. We have a blissful time, romping around on the floor, all thought of sermons momentarily forgotten.

The thought does return eventually, but simultaneously someone else arrives: my grandson, little Carl, the same age. More frolicking. And only after they leave, does it occur to me to go upstairs. I can hardly keep my eyes open, but then the Lord gives me a beautiful insight to share with the people tomorrow, and all's well.

That was the schedule into which I was now proposing to fit more speaking engagements. In my heart, I knew something was terribly wrong, and yet I didn't see how anything could be changed. Everything I was doing needed to be done. But I was getting more and more tired and irritable, under the unrelenting pressure.

But for all of my growing awareness of the tremendous strain that our life was putting on me, it never dawned on me how much strain it was putting on Mary—until it was almost too late.

CHAPTER SEVEN

The Breaking Point

I did not realize there was a crisis, that lovely morning in April of '78 when Mary asked me if I thought it would be all right if she visited her sister in Georgia, and her friend, Diane. I said sure, and went back to enjoying the fresh grapefruit that she had picked off our tree that morning. The Lord had blessed us with a grapefruit, an orange, and a lemon tree fifty feet from our back door, and we ate them as often as possible. Mary had never taken a trip on her own since we were married, but I obviously couldn't get away to go with her, and knowing how close she had been to her sister and to Diane, I was happy that she would have an opportunity to visit them. And so with no anxiety, about two weeks later, I drove Mary to San Diego to catch her flight for a one-week stay in Georgia.

One evening, a few days later, as Bruce and I finished a good meal that Genie had prepared, she asked, "When's Mom coming home?"

"Oh, I'm glad you brought that up," I replied,

deciding to tease her a little. "Your mother called this afternoon, and she's going to be staying another week."

"Another *week*?" Bruce groaned, and Genie's face fell.

"No," I said, smiling, "I was only kidding. She'll be home, the day after tomorrow." And they sighed with relief. Apparently, I was not as adept as Mary at managing the household.

That night, around ten, the phone rang. It was Mary, and her voice sounded strained. "Merlin, would it be all right if I stayed another week?" She paused. "No, let me put it another way: I really *need* to stay another week." And she ended, I heard what almost sounded like a choked-off sob.

"Well, of course you can. Don't think any more about it. We're doing fine. Get your tickets changed, and I'll meet the same plane a week later."

"Thanks," she said. "It's just that I—I need to stay awhile longer." And then she *was* crying.

"Okay, don't worry about a thing. Genie's doing a good job in the kitchen for fourteen years old, and Bruce is, you won't believe this, actually keeping his room picked up!" I exclaimed, hoping to coax a chuckle out of her.

But she wasn't in a laughing mood. "Well, give them my love. You, too."

"I love you, too, Mary. Now get a good night's sleep," I said inanely, because I couldn't think of anything else to say, "and you'll feel better in the morning."

When I had hung up, I shook my head and turned ⟵ back to the work on my desk. But later, lying in bed, I couldn't seem to get to sleep. I kept hearing that choked-off sob and the desperation in her voice. In all the years I had known her, Mary had never behaved this way. And then something else struck me: she had called at ten, which meant that it was one in the morning where she was. Something was wrong—*very* wrong.

I got up and knelt by the bed. I asked the Lord to forgive me for my insensitivity to Mary these past few months. I had gotten so involved in the various demands of my ministry, that the roof could have fallen in, and I wouldn't have noticed it. It dawned on me then, that could very well be what was about to happen. In the end, I praised God for the whole situation, but we both knew that my heart wasn't in it.

Hour after hour of the night passed, as I prayed and got up and paced the bedroom and then prayed some more. Finally, it got to be six o'clock, which meant that it was nine o'clock in Georgia and late enough to call. Mary was staying at her friend Diane's, who had been instrumental in her coming to the Lord, and who had remained a trusted Christian friend ever since. When Mary got on the phone, she was a little more her old self, but I sensed there was still a good deal of tension in her voice, and she hoped that my calling back didn't mean she couldn't stay the extra week. I assured her she could stay as long as she liked, and then wondered if I'd said the right thing. What if—I asked her if she could tell me what the trouble was.

"It started yesterday morning, when I woke up," she blurted out. "I couldn't get out of bed. I was paralyzed by the thought that in two more days, I would have to go home. I felt like a bird that had been let out of a cage, but someone had caught me and was fixing to put me back in that cage." An edge of desperation came back into her voice. "Inside the cage was this huge cat . . . it was lurking in there, licking its chops . . . just waiting for me to be put back in there!" And she fought back tears.

I tried to speak, but I couldn't. I felt like the wind had been knocked out of me. Mary sensed my reaction and tried to explain. "I guess it's been building up for a long time, but when I got out here and saw how peaceful these folks' lives are, and they love the Lord, too," the words came tumbling out now, in a rush, "and when I realized that there was another way to live, other than the wild, crazy pressure we're under all the time, something just sort of snapped. I tried praising God and fighting the dread, but it just got worse and worse, till finally I had to call you. I just couldn't bear leaving this peace and going back to that—" and she started to cry again.

I didn't know what to say. "Well, you take another week," I finally managed, "and when you come home, things will be different, I promise." But inside, I didn't see how they could be.

"I hope so, Merlin," she replied, and I sensed that she didn't really believe they would be either. "I hope so," she repeated, "because I just can't take it any more."

After we'd said goodbye, a heaviness came over me that increased as the day wore on. I struggled to praise God for this situation and the good that would come out of it, and what He was going to teach me through it, but all I could think of, over and over, was the uneasy awareness: *Mary doesn't want to come home at all.*

By evening, I was close to tears myself. For hours, I had wrestled the thing back and forth. I couldn't blame Mary; the way we were living *was* impossible. What's more, she had been trying to tell me that for months. On the other hand, I had a call of God on my life. It was an unusually demanding call, but I had known that when He had first called me, and I had accepted it. And, I knew that obedience to God had to come before all else.

But what of Mary's needs and the children's? Didn't they have a place in the call? Weren't we really called together? And yet, as I went over each facet of our life and my ministry for the umpteenth time, I did not see how I could do anything differently than I was already doing it. And I found myself being drawn deeper into despair. The situation seemed utterly insoluble.

And then Satan would whisper in my ear again: Mary does not want to come home at all. And he invited me to look at what might lie ahead, if things truly could not be changed.

By four in the morning, I was beside myself. For five hours I had tossed and turned in bed, resisting the urge to get up and phone. Around and around and around the paradox I went, until I had dug a circular trench in the ground of my mind, and my mind was capable of making the circuit without any conscious guidance on my part. With each lap, the trench grew a little deeper and made it that much harder to see any solution.

With sleep out of the question for the second night in a row, my nerves worn raw, and my anxiety acute, I was ready to listen to Satan, who summed up the alternatives succinctly: give up your ministry or lose your wife. And he would have been equally pleased with either decision. Enraged, I leaped out of bed and decided to take action. I didn't know what action I was going to take, but anything was better than lying in bed and listening to Old Slewfoot!

I threw some clothes in a suitcase and left a note for Bruce and Genie that I was catching a plane in San Diego, and for them to call a Christian friend of ours who always seemed to be available to come and stay with the kids whenever Mary and I had to go on a trip. And I muttered a prayer of praise to God, as I went out the garage door, that our two teen-agers had turned out to be so responsible.

Driving down Route 163 in the faint gray of pre-dawn, I felt a little better that I was at least on my way, even if I didn't know where. In the back of my mind was the thought that maybe I could arrange all the connections and get to Georgia that evening, in spite of the three-hour time loss. But on the other hand, I had no assurance that Mary would even want to see me. Well, I was going *somewhere,* and I would just leave it up to God to show me where, when I got to the airport.

I'm acting crazy, I told myself, but even as I did so, I began to relax. A navigator was useless to a ship, as long as the ship was tied up at the dock. But once the ship had slipped its mooring and was underway, then the navigator could guide it. I sensed that somehow God was in this; in fact, I was aware of His presence in the car with me.

When I got to the airport, I seemed to get a nudge to go to the United Airlines counter, and there I found that by "coincidence," I was just in time for a flight to Chicago that would connect with an afternoon flight to Columbus, Georgia. I could reach Mary by nightfall! And now, for the first time since Mary's call two days before, I was able to praise God and really mean it!

On the plane, I felt a peace settle over me, like I hadn't known in days—or weeks, for that matter. I didn't know what I was going to do, or what I was going to say, but in my heart I sensed that, however far down the road it might be, God was going to work things out. And that was so wonderful that I was even able to sleep.

When I reached Columbus, I called Mary from the airport, and asked her how she was doing. She said she felt a little better. She didn't say anything about changing her mind about the second week.

"Well, would you like to see me?" I asked, suddenly fearing a listless response.

"Why? Where are you?" she asked, and my heart leaped at the excitement in her voice.

"Oh, I'm at the airport," I replied, trying to sound casual.

"Where?"

"In San Diego," I answered, asking God to forgive me for the lie.

"Oh," her voice fell.

That was all the encouragement I needed. "Look, if I can work out the connections, would you like me to come and see you?"

"Could you?"

"I don't know, but I'll try, if you really want me to."

"Oh, please come! Come right away!" and now she was really excited.

"Okay, I'll do my best." There were tears in my eyes, as I hung up the phone and left the booth. Now where were the rent-a-cars? I don't think O.J. Simpson made it any faster to the Hertz desk than I did that evening. I got the directions I needed and was soon driving through the Georgia dusk, singing every hymn I could think of.

When I pulled into the driveway, Diane happened to catch sight of me out the window and slipped out to meet me in the yard. Giving me a big hug, as if she hadn't seen me in years, she put her finger to her lips and led me quietly into the living room. Then she looked into the kitchen and said, "Mary, can you come here a moment?"

Mary came in, wiping her hands on an apron. "I still haven't figured out where you keep your salt and pepper shakers," she said apologetically, then she looked up and her eyes widened. "Merlin!" she shouted and ran to me, throwing her arms around me. We held each other so tight, we could barely breathe.

I took her out to dinner then, even though she had already eaten, and we talked and talked, like a couple of kids. The next day we spent walking in a beautiful floral park, not talking much now, just holding hands and enjoying the fragrance and beauty of the flowers all around us. It was so peaceful there, so warm and fragrant and beautiful, that I imagined Eden must have been something like it. And, we felt God was close to us—very close, though neither of us knew what it was that He was trying to teach us. This much we did know: He was able and all we had to do was trust Him, and keep listening.

The next day, I had to leave for a five-day crusade in southern Massachusetts and Rhode Island. But I left with a heart brimful of hope and joy and praise. I was sure now that God was about to speak to me and show me what needed to be done.

He did speak to me, but not in the way that I was expecting, for I had unwittingly entered one of the most grueling ordeals of my life. There were three or four meetings scheduled every day, each in a different town. At each one, I spoke and then prayed for people afterwards, and we drive from town to town in a mini-compact with four people in it, spending as much as five hours a day just traveling. It would be very late when I finally got to bed and very early when we got going again the next day to keep on schedule.

On each speaking occasion, at the last minute, the Lord's grace would descend, and His Spirit would anoint me and speak through me and the other speaker who was sharing this crusade. Thousands were being blessed and hundreds were accepting Christ, but I was getting so tired I could hardly think. Every bone in my body ached, and then I realized that at fifty-three, I was not exactly young any more.

As one day blurred into the next, I became increasingly aware that changes simply *had* to be made when I got home. I tried to listen to God, but I was too tired to hear what it was He was trying to tell me.

CHAPTER • EIGHT

Pulling Back

On the plane back to California, I dozed fitfully, too tired and keyed up to relax. One thing consoled me: Mary would be home when I got there. That first night we had together in Georgia, I had told her that I was sure the Lord was saying that she wouldn't have to appear with me on television any more, or minister with me on crusades. And she was tremendously relieved. She had participated because I had wanted her to, as I had wanted her to share every aspect of my life.

A number of months back, I began to see the extra pressure such appearances were putting on her, and that she was telling the truth when she said how little she enjoyed them. So at that time I had left it up to her to decide whether or not she would come. But instead of helping matters, I had only made them worse. Now, if she stayed home she felt guilty, knowing that I was hoping she would want to come.

But finally, somewhere between Chicago and Atlanta, God had gotten through to me that Mary's call was different than mine. She was called to a supporting role—to care for our children and our home, as God intended, and to care for me, too, which included continuing to tell me where and when she felt I was not hearing God, or that something was wrong. It was wrong for me to have put the burden of deciding on her shoulders.

So, I had told her, and she was so grateful that I wondered why it had taken me so long to see it. And now, flying home on the plane, I anticipated a new atmosphere of peace around our house, because Mary had been released.

When I got home that afternoon, she *did* look rested—which was not exactly how I appeared to her. "Merlin!" she exclaimed, "you look half dead! As soon as you've said hello to the children, why don't you go upstairs and take a nap?" And I gratefully did as she suggested.

The next day, however, I was right back in the old routine. When I went down to the office, I found that the situation there had gotten worse than ever. Not only was the computer totally nonproductive, it almost seemed to be mocking us, while unanswered correspondence was piling ever higher. The staff was under such pressure that they were getting tense and edgy, and what was my solution?

Everyone would simply have to work harder, and I would set the example. I started coming in early and working late, and the rest of the staff did likewise. In effect, I was putting us on an emergency footing, calling for a maximum all-out effort, until we were over the hump. And they turned to and performed as well as any commander could ask for.

The trouble was, we never did seem to get over the hump. The hump seemed to go on forever, and every solution that I came up with was merely a stopgap measure, and about as effective. Nothing ever really got *solved*. My solution? To work harder than ever. But the harder I worked, the more things seemed to go wrong.

And now Mary, seeing the enormous strain I was under, began to get frustrated again. She would try to tell me that I was going to ruin my health if I kept it up, and that there didn't seem to be any of the peace of God in the way that I was working. On the contrary, perhaps things were going so wrong, not in spite of my working so hard, but because of it. But I kept explaining that there was nothing else to do. And so, she stopped trying to get me to listen, and her lips were more and more frequently compressed in a thin line.

This time, I could see it coming. I knew I was driving her to that point of total frustration again, and I was driving myself there, too. No matter what I did, it went wrong. I was crying out to God constantly but my mind was in such a state of anxiety that I knew I couldn't hear the Holy Spirit, no matter how much I wanted to.

Finally, after a horrible day in which I had woken up irritated and snapped at everyone in my family and in the office, I knew I had to do something. So I did something that I heard of others doing, but had never done myself. Availing myself of a secluded hideaway on the Pacific Coast which we had access to, I went there alone, to stay for three days of fasting and prayer. It was the only thing left to do.

As soon as I got there, I got down on my knees and cried out to God for about half an hour, telling Him all the things that were wrong, and asking Him what to do. But such was the turmoil in my spirit, there was no way I could hear Him, even if He had chosen to answer me. So, I got up off my knees and went for a walk on the beach.

I walked south for miles, listening to the waves as they crashed on the shore and eddied around my ankles, and watching the sun dance on the surface of the deep blue-green breakers. Where I had started walking, there were many vacationers enjoying the ocean, a few with small body-surfing boards, most just bobbing up and down in place, or holding ecstatic little children just above the waves. But after a couple of hours of walking, the busy beaches were far behind, and a few wheeling and cavorting gulls were all there were to keep me company.

Not that I was in want of companionship; my mind was still too keyed up. But walking by the oceanside was having its effect. Even though I was not consciously aware of any change, my heart began to relax, and I began to believe that God was going to speak to me before the three days were up. In the meantime, I began to enjoy my surroundings, as I had not enjoyed them for—how long? With the exception of that brief interlude in Georgia with Mary, I could not remember when I last had simply enjoyed being immersed in the full splendor of God's natural creation!

But now, step by step as I walked along the firm, wet sand, under that glorious hazy blue sky and felt the hot sun loosening my muscles, that appreciation began to seep back into me. And I began to be grateful to be alive—to be God's child—and to know that He had put all this beauty here on earth for us to share with Him. The tang of the salt air, the cry of a gliding gull, the sparkle of a white sail on the horizon, the cotton candy shape of a small cumulus cloud scudding inland, the contrast of the hot, soft dry sand a few feet to my left, and the hard-packed wet sand I was walking on—all these things seemed to flow together—interwoven harmonies in a symphony of peace.

The sun was now well out over the ocean to the west, when I turned around and headed back. Sometimes I could find my tracks, sometimes they were washed away, and as I looked up, the beach seemed to disappear in the distance, in a milky, blue-white haze. On and on I walked, there was no hurry, and by the time I returned to my starting place, there was perhaps an hour left before the sun would sink into the ocean. The once-busy beaches were almost deserted now; most families had gone home. A little fellow in a big snorkle mask that had obscured his lateral vision bumped into me, as he hurried out of the surf in response to a parental summons. I grinned and tousled his hair and pointed him in the direction of his waiting father.

I slept well that night—no dreams, no tormenting anxieties, no mental pacing. I knew God would speak to me, when He was ready—correction when *I* was ready—and in the meantime, I just relaxed and waited.

The next day, I walked again. This time I found myself noticing things that I had been oblivious to the day before—the way the wind as well as the ocean sculpted the sand, how every ninth wave seemed a little larger than the rest, how there were some quite extraordinary shells to be found, if one had the patience to watch for them. I picked up some unusual ones for Mary and Genie; they were a delicate pink shade and exquisitely formed, though you couldn't hear the ocean very well in them. But somehow this didn't seem to matter. Their beauty was reason enough for their creation.

That afternoon, having returned from my excursion along the beach, I rested. As I breathed in the quietness that pervaded the atmosphere, I realized that God was speaking to me in a still, small voice. In the quietness of my spirit He said one word: *Rest.*

I started to get excited that at last I was hearing from Him again, and I had a long list of questions I wanted to ask Him, but all He would say was *rest*.

Lord, what do you want me to do, specifically, regarding Praise Center and our plan to build a new church?

Rest.

It wasn't until much later that evening, as I sat out on the little balcony and watched the night ocean gently breaking on the sand under a clear, starry sky, that I finally began to understand what He meant: *I don't want you to do anything. I want you to take your hands completely off of it, and let Roy and the elders who have been called by me solve those problems.*

All right, Lord, that's what I'll do. But what about the foundation?

Rest.

And it turned out, He meant essentially the same thing. *Do nothing. Turn it over to Marilyn Wyman, whom I have called. Let her manage the foundation office, and let me speak through her.*

And what would you have me do, regarding Mary?

Rest. Trust her completely into my care.

And that was it. As grateful as I was to finally receive clear and explicit direction from God, when I woke up the next morning, I was surprised to note that I did not have a sense of peace inside, as I had expected. So, I did some more praying and some more listening. And I began to see why: subconsciously, I did not *want* to just let go of everything. Apparently, deep down in my heart, I somehow felt my self-worth was tied up in my work. I felt that I was integral to its success, even indispensable.

And so, the third day, I heard quite a bit from the Lord, and not all of it was pleasant. In the thirty years I had spent in the ministry, I had always worked hard and done everything that was asked of me, as far as was humanly possible. I was proud of the fact that I had always given myself totally to whatever project I had become involved in, and now God was asking me—no, telling me—to let it all go.

Well, I would, I assured the Lord, but I felt a twinge of self-pity at the same time. And immediately, I heard in my heart the scriptural promise that Jesus had sent His Spirit to be not just our teacher and our director and guide, but our comforter.

Well, Father, I know that's what your Word says, but I'm afraid that at the moment, I don't feel particularly comforted.

And then in my heart I heard God say very distinctly: *Do you believe my Son? Do you believe what He has told you? Do you believe His Spirit is your comforter?*

And I made a choice. By an act of my will, I chose to *believe* that the Holy Spirit was my comforter. At that instant, it seemed that all the problems of the past weeks and months were suddenly gone. My spirit was set free.

With an amazing sense of release, and more

light-hearted than I had felt in years, I drove back to Escondido. I went to the office, and shared with Roy and Marilyn what the Lord had shown me. Despite all the problems the foundation faced, despite the fact that in myself I felt like a deserter, abandoning them in the trenches under fire, as it were, that was what the Lord had said to do, and that was what I was going to do.

To my surprise and great joy, both of them responded with smiles of delight. "Merlin," Roy beamed, "I *know* that's the Lord! I've been wishing you would do something like this for a long time. We accept all the responsibilities, don't we, Marilyn?"

She nodded, tears of joy in her eyes. "Go home and rest and listen to the Lord and fellowship with Him, and get that channel between you and Him clear and open! There's no way that you can do or be what you're called to, unless you stay in close harmony with Him. If you don't, a lot of people are going to miss out!"

So it was set. I would come back tomorrow with some specific recommendations regarding the foundation, and then would not officially be back in the office until the Lord indicated that I was to get re-involved.

At home, Mary's reaction was also delight. "You mean, after all these years, we are really going to get a chance to be a family again? Hallelujah!"

The next day, when I went back to the office, I informed Roy and Marilyn that the Lord seemed to be telling me to get rid of the computer. I had not yet seen the why of it, I explained, but this was where our troubles had begun. Roy and Marilyn witnessed most emphatically to the returning of the computer, and no sooner had we finished discussing it, than Marilyn called the computer company and told them that since they had not fulfilled any of their promises or commitments, we wanted them to pick up their machine immediately.

But getting rid of the computer was not going to be that easy. The company said, "Fine, we'll pick it up, only it's going to cost you half the purchase price, payable immediately."

Well, that was not what the Lord had told us. We agreed to forfeit our down payment, but that was all. For several days, they called with counter-proposals, but we remained firm, though our lawyer advised us that we didn't have better than a fifty-fifty chance of winning our case, should it ever go to court. For a while it was a stalemate, but finally the computer company accepted our terms.

And so, one afternoon, Marilyn called with good news: "I know you said that you weren't coming into the office, but I wondered if you might want to come down, off the record, just to watch the beautiful sight that is about to unfold here. You see, there's this big red truck parked out back, and there are these three men here, busily dis-installing the computer, and—"

Before she could finish, I was on my way downtown. I got there in time to see that gleaming, impressive electronic millstone going out the door.

At Praise Center, we have a traditional way of celebrating a joyous occasion. We form a circle and join hands and sing, "My Feet Have Got the Message; They're Filled with Joy and Praise," hopping twice on the left foot and twice on the right, and then clapping our hands to keep time. Even King David could not have danced before the Lord with more exuberance than we did that afternoon!

CHAPTER • NINE

Listening

Pulling back was easier, once the computer was gone. In fact, it was so easy that I wondered why I had thought it would be so hard. I was even a little dismayed; apparently I was not as indispensable as I had thought. Trinity Broadcasting called to see how soon I could start another series of daily broadcasts, and when I told them what the Lord had told me, instead of being disappointed, they said, "Fine, take all the rest you need. Actually, it's good programing to have a break between the series."

At Praise Center, people were disappointed that I wouldn't be preaching or involved in church activities for a season, but they understood the need for a sabbatical. And what a relief not to have to worry about a sermon every Sunday.

At the foundation, Marilyn soon lined up another local business which had its own computer and would work out a time-sharing arrangement with us. So in effect we were back where we had been eight months before, only this time with a company which was glad to have us use their equipment.

Perhaps the hardest thing of all was to cancel all my speaking engagements for three months. But there, too, people understood. In their own lives, they had had crises, and they could appreciate the need for my heeding the Lord's bidding. Wherever possible, I told them that as soon as I could resume my crusades, I would consider them first.

And so, in a matter of days, I was completely extricated. Free. Without a care in the world. It was such an unusual sensation that at first I gave in to just enjoying it. I began to once more hear the birds in the palm tree beside our home. I took an interest in our fruit trees, especially the new plum tree which was bearing fruit after only two years. It needed pruning and watering, and I delighted in working with my hands around the place, spending as much time outdoors as possible.

And we started doing things together as a family, whether it was just going out to dinner, or to the Wild Animal Park, or more involved excursions, like camping in the desert, or a raft trip down the Colorado River. I became genuinely interested in what my son and daughter were doing. Bruce, like his older brothers, was a car buff, and like them, he had the mechanical ingenuity to take an engine down, bolt by bolt until every last part was disassembled, and then mill its heads and get it back together again. He had bought a former late-model stock car for $100 and a wrecked car with a good engine of the same model and vintage, and was proceeding to cannibalize the latter for the sake of the former. My only objection was that this was taking place in the back yard. But Bruce was a "perseverer," and I was confident he would see the job through.

Genie, on the other hand, was learning to sew and play semi-classical music on the piano—two things a father could do little more than express approval of. But that helped; she knew that I really cared. And every evening, Mary and I would go for a two-mile walk together, after supper. That walk was her favorite part of the day, she told me, and it's funny how close two people can grow, just sharing little things like that.

My fellowship with the Lord was growing, too. I was beginning to hear the Holy Spirit as I had not heard Him for years. He was my teacher again, pointing out truths and insights and revelations in an almost unbroken stream. It was awesome. And so much of my life had been given to preparing a sermon or a speech for a television message or something for a book, that whenever He showed me something remarkable, my first impulse was to hurry and find pencil and paper and write it down. It would make a gem of a sermon illustration one day.

But each time, I started to do this, the Lord would say, *Rest. You are to learn, not write. I will recall to your mind anything you might need in the future. What you are to do now is learn of me, and renew fellowship with me.* So, sheepishly I would comply, and gradually the lessons shifted from the head level down to the heart level. And listening became experiencing.

One of the most moving things that I experienced was the depth of His love for me—the infinite patience which He had shown me in the past, when I had had no time for Him, or no desire to listen. The care that He was taking to show me, before He moved on to the next lesson. And I was stunned, the day I realized that He considered it more important that I abide in Him, than change the world for Him, in any way. And He wanted me to regard my fellowship with Him, above anything I did for the rest of my life.

As I became more and more aware with each passing day of how much God loved me, I began to feel a new love for God. I loved Him. I was rediscovering that I could fellowship with Him—not as a "director," who outlined the work I was to accomplish, but as a counselor, to whom I could come, and sit at His feet and talk things over with, and be strengthened and renewed.

And as I came into this new relationship with the Lord, a new understanding of praise began to come to me, slowly at first, then more clearly. I had always taught people that the secret of putting praise to work in their lives was to be willing to praise God in *all* circumstances (1 Thess. 5:18), especially when that was the last thing they felt like doing. But now I was beginning to see that there was something more.

It is important to praise God, no matter what has befallen us, and indeed, we are commanded to do no less (Eph. 5:20). God knows very well how hard it is for us to praise Him at such times; He knows that it is by an act of our will that we do so (Heb. 13:15), against all the desires of our natural self. And especially against all human reasoning, but God honors obedience. Often, that one clenched-teeth act of obedience will be sufficient to put in motion all the mighty machinery of divine intervention. Often it is the key that opens the door for a loving God to act on our behalf, as is promised in His Word: "All things work together for good to them that love God, to them who are the called according to his purpose" (Rom. 8:28). *Those who love God*—if we love Him, then we should be willing to praise Him, regardless of the circumstances (Eph. 5:20). Sometimes that praise was mechanical, sometimes it was grudging, but God took that into account, and if we persisted, often He would provide the grace to change our feelings and transform it into sincere praise.

But now I was seeing—experiencing—a new dimension of praise. It was spontaneous praise that just sort of bubbled up, unbidden, from the heart. It rose like living water from the wellspring of a grateful heart. It is this spontaneous praise that most delights the heart of God.

Two of the stepping stones to having an abidingly grateful heart (as opposed to the flashes of dazzling gratitude that most of us have experienced), a heart running over with the love of God, could be found in the refrain of that wonderful old camp-meeting song, "Trust and Obey." If we will obey Him, even when He says let go of everything, even our most cherished dreams, we may very soon be surprised to find praise overflowing in our hearts.

In my own case, I realized that I needed to turn over the problem of the foundation and the church to the Lord, not just in my mind but in my heart, so that I *knew* deep down that they belonged to God, and were not my burden. That did not mean that I was to work any less, when I went back on a regular schedule. It simply meant that from now on, my work would be controlled by Him, the way it should have been, all along.

Meditating on that, I began to see that God has cycles that each of our lives go through. The Holy Spirit caused me to remember back when I was in college. I worked thirty hours a week in a metal foundry, *and* took twenty-two hours of classes a week, which was actually more than the college allowed. Nor was that all: I had a second job, cleaning the latrines in our trailer camp. I worked nonstop the whole week, and the only free time I had was on Sunday.

But Sundays were nonstop, too. After church, I would go down to the local jail and hold a service there. (I was so "on fire for the Lord" in those days, it was a miracle that more inmates got saved than singed!) On Sunday afternoons, I went up and down the streets, passing out tracts and witnessing to anyone who would stop and listen. For the call on my life, as I understood it at that time, was to use every possible opportunity to win people for Christ. I felt the Lord was telling me: *If you ever have a chance to tell someone about me, do it. Don't be embarrassed, don't deny me. And if you are ever asked to speak, do it.*

I heeded that call, through seminary, throughout my chaplaincy in the army and my time as a Methodist minister. Naturally, I assumed that this meant I would continue to do so for the rest of my life. But when *Prison to Praise* became a bestseller, there were soon more speaking invitations than I could possibly accept. The time came when I was only able to accept one in ten, then one in twenty, then one in sixty. I had a growing sense of guilt, because I felt I was somehow not fulfilling the call God had given me, even though it was now physically impossible.

Finally, the Holy Spirit straightened out my thinking on that score. God takes us through one phase in our walk with Him, during which He gives us an opportunity to show that we are willing to do anything and everything that He would ask of us—any place, any time, under any circumstances. But then there comes a point where He leads us into a different phase in our walk with Him, and somewhat belatedly I was recognizing that this was what had been taking place in my own life.

I realized that God was now saying something else

to me: *I am pleased with the intent of your heart, but you are trying to do all these things in your own strength, driving yourself, and this is not what I have called my children to do. I have called them to abide in me. I have called them to be filled with my peace. How can you share my peace with the world, when you do not possess it yourself?*

Father, I groaned, does this mean that all this time I have been trying to be obedient to your call on my life, but. . . .

Did you think that I was calling you to do all those things? I was not, because you cannot do them. But when you are abiding in my peace, then you will be able to do anything. Because it will not be you doing it. It will be me doing it through you.

Which did not mean I was to just put my feet up and leave it all up to God, or act in any manner irresponsibly. When the time came, I would be working just as hard, but with one great difference. The burden would be the Lord's, not mine. And the moment I began to feel anxious in my spirit, or felt the pressure beginning to rise, that would be a sure sign that God's peace had slipped away from me, and it was time to stop and listen.

Already, as I write this I have begun to resume some of my activities—in the office, preaching on Sundays, and so on. And I will be doing increasingly more in weeks to come. But there is a peace inside now—a peace that was never there before. It is a precious peace, which resides deep in my spirit, and which I treasure.

Unbidden praise was frequently on my lips, and although I didn't think so at first, perhaps the happiest surprise of all was to discover just how unnecessary my strivings were and to see the fruit of my pulling back for a season. God was right: it was Him, all along!

In the meantime, I was enjoying the first real time off that I had had since our trip to Southern California, six years before. At that time, we had gone pack-riding up into the Grand Teton Mountains in Wyoming. This time, in July, we were going back to the wilderness. But where we had gone up before, now we were going down—down a mile deep into the Colorado River Canyon, and then down that river on a six-day raft trip.

CHAPTER • TEN

Down in the Valley

On the morning of July 11, the Carothers family was scheduled to embark on a six-day adventure down the Green and Colorado rivers. We would be joined by Roy and Marilyn, and their two teen-age sons, who would meet us on the evening of the tenth, at a motel in Green River, Utah. They were driving, and left early on the morning of the ninth, to be sure to get there on time, as it was thirteen hours by car. I would be flying our family in, as it took only three and one-half hours by air.

We almost didn't make it; a twenty-four-hour flu bug was going around Escondido, and it bit Mary the night before we were due to leave. Yet even though she felt terrible, she was confident it would quickly pass, and was determined not to miss the trip we had been looking forward to for so long. And so, as we boarded the little Cessna at Palomar airport, she settled into the back seat with Genie and was asleep almost before we left the runway.

It was perfect flying weather—CAVU, as the

military used to call it: Ceiling Absolute, Visibility Unlimited. Bruce was in the co-pilot's seat, and as soon as we had leveled off at ten thousand feet, I turned the controls over to him, pleased at the maturity he was demonstrating. I gave him a course that would take us over Bryce National Park, and settled back to enjoy the scenery.

From the air, Bryce Canyon was even more spectacular than I had anticipated. There were vast, deep cuts in the ground, some of them as deep as a fair-sized mountain was high, and the sides of the canyon were varied in hue, from a light, dusty sand color, to deep purple.

Suddenly, though the air was perfectly clear, the plane started bucking like a rodeo bull. With no warning, we were thrust two hundred feet up in the air, as if we were in an elevator that went from the first to the twentieth floor in three seconds. Then, just as suddenly, we would be dropped two hundred feet, with the wings shuddering on impact, as we hit the bottom of the air pocket.

"Updrafts," I called to Bruce over the noise of the engine, and I took over the controls. "Nothing to worry about." But in the back seat I heard Genie praying.

We got over Bryce without further incident and began our descent for Green River. But finding the field was another matter. After much trying, I managed to raise someone on the ground, who told me approximately where the landing strip was:

tucked between a highway and a railroad track that were roughly parallel one another. I found the highway and the railroad track, but the strip, which was marked down on my chart as asphalt, must have gotten covered with sand, because it was nowhere to be seen. Nevertheless, now saying a prayer myself, I started down. I lined up with where the runway was supposed to be, but frankly the broad empty highway to the left looked far more inviting! Right up until touchdown, I was not sure whether I was going to wind up on the road or the airstrip, but as it turned out, my ground information was right, and we made a surprisingly smooth landing, right where we were supposed to be.

That evening, at dinner, Mary felt up to sitting with us as we ate, though she still had no desire for food herself. Not our Genie, though. The plane trip, and the ride in the truck that the motel had sent for us, had given her an outdoors appetite, and she ordered a huge plate of spaghetti. Mary shuddered at the sight of it. "Genie, I just hope you don't get the bug tonight. If you do, you'll never eat spaghetti again!"

It was pretty late before we finally turned out the light, but about fifteen minutes later, there was a groan, and the patter of feet to the bathroom. Mary's spaghetti observation had turned out to be prophetic. Genie was sick throughout the night, and by morning she was so wrung out that it was all we could do to rally her spirits.

For two hours, we bounced along in a homemade, un-air-conditioned bus, and finally arrived at the Green River, where I could see the four rafts, all loaded with provisions. They were enormous! Twelve feet long, with a cross-seat in each for an oarsman, they were completely surrounded by huge yellow rubber tubes, inflated to a full two feet in diameter. At the sight of them, everyone grew excited; the sparkle returned to Mary's eye, and even Genie perked up.

We got into our rafts, the thrill of adventure gripping us all. Our leader, Dee Holliday, and his wife, Sue, were in the first raft. In our raft, a cheerful man named Temple was at the oars. Roy and I were in the bow, and Mary and Marilyn had settled comfortably in the stern. In the next raft were our kids, and a couple of other families were in the remaining raft. Shortly after ten, we waved goodbye to the bus driver and cast off. The water beneath us was smooth, but running swiftly; I estimated that we were drifting at a fast walking pace—a little faster than a man could walk, actually, but not as fast as he could run.

It was an eerie feeling to be gliding along in silence, the only sound being the occasional dip of an oar to keep us in the center of the current. All of us were awestruck by the spectacle of the towering, multi-layered, dun-colored cliffs that rose on either side of us, with an avenue of sky far above, so blue that if I had a photo of it, no one would believe it. The sun was high enough now to reach down into the gorge, leaving one wall in dark shadow, the other in blazing light. It struck me that we were being taken through a giant cathedral that God himself had carved out eons ago, and as we left all signs of civilization far behind, I felt my scalp tighten; it was as if we were going backwards in time.

For about an hour, we glided along in this manner, a hush that was almost reverential pervading our little band. Around one bend, and then the next, each scene was different from the one before, and each was breathtaking in its majesty. My senses were freely drinking in the beauty that met us at each turn of the river. This first hour was worth the entire trip!

The sun was approaching its zenith now, and it was getting quite hot, despite the coolness of the snow-fed river beneath us. Out of the corner of my eye, I noticed that the raft with the kids in it was pulling closer to us; presumably, the oarsman wanted a word with Temple. When they had gotten within a few feet of us, suddenly the young people whooped like wild Indians and deluged us with water from bailing buckets and plastic pails, shrieking with laughter. Looking at their faces contorted with glee, I imagined that must have been what pirates looked like as they swung aboard a helpless merchantman. We pleaded for mercy, and after they relented, I whispered to Temple to make sure we had some buckets that afternoon, after lunch. Such a dastardly assault would not go unavenged!

We stopped for lunch on one of the sandy strips of beach that could be found on the inside banks of broader curves in the river. Setting up a sandwich smorgasbord with all the makings, so that each one could create his own epicurean delight, the crew also provided a cooler full of cold drinks, and large jugs of fresh water or lemonade. It was quite a spread, and I hadn't realized how hungry and thirsty I was. Downing one glass of lemonade and then another, I made myself a generous and thoroughly delicious peanut butter and jelly sandwich, studding the peanut butter with a generous quantity of plump raisins. I devoured the sandwich, considered another, but decided on a couple of large handfuls of salted peanuts instead.

That afternoon, as we drifted along, I pulled an old hat down over my eyes, to shield them from the alternating bright sun and dark shadows, and yielded myself to a delightful snooze. When I awoke and noticed that the kids in the other raft were still napping, I leaned over to Temple and suggested that the time might be ripe for a counterattack. He nodded, a mischievous twinkle in his eye. Moving slowly so as not to attract attention, we all filled the buckets on the side of the raft which could not be seen, and Temple eased us toward the other raft. It was impossible to keep from grinning; I felt like Captain Hornblower sneaking up on a heavily armed but unsuspecting British man-of-war.

Surely, they must see us; we were less than thirty

feet away, and closing! But they all seemed to be asleep; even their oarsman seemed to have been lulled into drowsiness. Twenty feet—fifteen—ten—Marilyn, Mary, Roy and I brought our buckets to the ready. Now their oarsman saw us, but before he could raise the alarm, I cried, "Now!" Their quiet reveries were inundated by a torrent of water. So complete was their surprise, that we were able to get off several broadsides before they could bring any of their buckets into action. Such sputtering and jostling as they frantically tried to return as good as they got! We all got drenched but it was worth it!

Along about five, we came to a narrow sandbank, which was where we would camp for the night. On the land side of the sandbank was a marsh which, two of our number discovered, would not support human weight, as they sank into the smelly ooze up to their hips. That meant we were confined to this short, narrow strip of sand until departure in the morning.

Supper was a cook-out, par excellence—rib-eye steaks cooked on a grill over a wood fire, with all the trimmings—and for dessert, strawberry shortcake! The aroma of those steaks beginning to cook caused everyone's tastebuds to tingle with anticipation—except for me; all of a sudden, the aroma was having the reverse effect, causing me to lose all appetite. Increasingly aware that all was not well in my inner regions, I moved to the farthest edge of the sandbank to escape the savory smells of supper.

Unfortunately, I could not escape the now decidedly unsavory taste of the lemonade and peanuts, peanut butter, jelly and raisins, which had been great at high noon. And in that last moment before I was sick, like a drowning man reviewing his life, my whole lunch passed before my eyes.

I was sick as a dog! Over and over again, into the river, unfortunately only a few feet from the rest of the party. Crawling back to my sleeping bag, and grateful for Mary's help, I got in and tried to rest. But in a little while, I was back at the edge of the bank again. I felt so awful, I was afraid I was dying. But in a little while, I felt so awful, I was afraid I *wasn't* dying!

I spent the next day curled up in a ball, in the stern of the raft, my hat pulled far down over my eyes, drifting in and out of sleep.

Evening found us camped on another sandbank, and I had finally revived enough to sit up and look around. I still didn't want anything to eat, but I had the strangest desire for a cup of coffee—strange, because I hardly ever drank coffee! At first, I tried to talk myself into something more sensible, but the desire was persistent, so Mary gave me some coffee. My spirits picked up noticeably with that cup, and I rejoined the land of the living.

The next morning, although still a bit shaky as a result of not having eaten anything for nearly two hectic days, I suddenly experienced a hearty appetite. Fried eggs and blueberry pancakes never tasted so good!

A few hours later we arrived at Cataract Canyon, where the Green River joins the mighty Colorado. Up until fifteen years ago, Cataract Canyon was impossible to navigate. A few men had tried it in wooden boats and had tragically lost their lives when their craft had been dashed to pieces in the churning waters. And this was the same white water towards which we were now heading. Though the surface of the river was still deceptively smooth, we had picked up speed and were now moving a good deal faster that a man could run.

If the walls of the Green River Canyon were impressive, the sides of Cataract Canyon were mind-boggling. They extended 1500 to 2000 feet almost straight up, and the sky above seemed like a mere ribbon of blue. Dee Holliday has done some extensive research on the canyon, and he had informed me that, according to geologists, it had taken 26 million years for the canyon to be formed.

"How much deeper has it grown since the time of Christ?" I asked.

"Oh, about six inches," was Dee's reply.

All along the canyon, Temple pointed out to us faint traces of the Anazazi Indian tribe, who were known to have left the area fifteen hundred years ago. Since that time, until the advent of these raft trips, the only men to have been there were a few desperate outlaws who had used the canyon as a hideout. Ahead, somewhere beyond the next few bends, we began to hear a distant roaring. "That," Dee shouted to the other rafts, "is the sound of white water. Everyone make sure that your life preservers are well fastened, and if your raft goes over don't panic. Stay under the raft, where an air pocket will provide plenty of air to breathe. Or, if you get separated, grab a breath every time your life preserver bobs you to the surface, and just be patient until you get to the end of that stretch of white water, when we'll scoop you up."

We rounded one bend and then another, and suddenly, there it was! The water was white, all right; a creamy spray filled the air as water billowed over huge hidden boulders.

Temple was a picture of steely concentration now as he steered the raft for the first inverted "V," where rushing waters squeezed between two giant boulders lurking just beneath the surface. No sooner would we shoot through one "V," then we would row like mad to avoid a boulder dead ahead, and get us into the next "V." Later, I learned that if a raft ever did go up on one of those boulders, the force of the water coming behind it was so great that it would flip the raft end over end.

As the rafts entered the first surging white water, all the women screamed, and most of us men did too—not from fear, but out of sheer exhilaration. Everywhere I looked, there was flying spray, blinding white where it caught the sun, and all we could hear was the thundering roar of the rapids. Up and down and around we went. The first impression was one of complete chaos. After the initial impact of riding into the white waters, I became aware that though the tempest tossed us about with a vengeance, the captain at the helm of our little craft was in control—now steering, now rowing, now watching to see exactly what Dee was doing in his raft in front of us, and, with split-second precision, avoiding the hidden boulders.

Too soon, the day's series of rapids was over, and it was time to make camp. That evening, around the campfire, we had a time of fellowship that was the best of the trip thus far. The perils we had shared—and survived—drew us into a unity of spirit that enveloped our little group like the warmth of our glowing campfire.

Just before supper was ready, I went on a little exploring trip into an adjacent canyon that had once been carved out by a tributary, long since dried up. Dusk was already beginning to settle in down where we were, and the further I went back into the dim recesses of that old canyon, the stronger I felt an awareness, a stillness—something almost supernatural. Walking slowly, not to disturb this stillness, I went as far in as it was possible to go, perhaps 300 feet. And then, I stood still—and waited. I had the feeling that something was going to happen, as if I were there by appointment. If this were a movie, the background music would now be reaching a crescendo which would have produced tremendous suspense! But this was real, I reminded myself. By now, I could barely move, the sensation was so strong, and I held my breath, waiting. I didn't know what I was waiting for—what was going to happen; was the Lord about to appear to me? Nothing happened. Ten minutes, fifteen minutes—nothing.

Perplexed, I went back to camp and asked Mary to go with me along that same route. By now it was quite dim in the canyon and we had to tread our way carefully. As we proceeded, Mary too felt the same sense of expectancy I had picked up, only it struck her a little differently; she half-expected to see a flying saucer coming zooming out of the far reaches of the canyon. We went all the way back in, but still nothing happened. Finally, we returned to the campsite.

At dinner, Dee told us that one of the other oarsmen, Tim, would take any of us who were interested—and ambitious enough to get up at five-thirty—into the canyon and up one of its sides. I was the first to volunteer, but my enthusiastic response was prompted not so much by the exciting prospect of getting up before the sun, but the firm conviction that God had some revelation for me in there.

So, in the half-light of predawn, six of us filed after our guide as he led us back up the canyon. When he reached what I thought had to be the end, he began to work his way back and forth up the canyon wall, finding narrow ledges and passages hidden from the uninitiated eye. As we began our ascent up this seemingly impassable mountain of rock, with sheer drops at every turn, the silence was broken only by the labored breathing of six indomitable spirits bent on scaling the heights.

Higher and higher we climbed, and again I had an overpowering sense of spiritual awareness. After about an hour, Tim paused and had us look back down into the canyon. Several of us gasped; we had not realized how high we had climbed. As we surveyed the scene far below, the rafts were no bigger than yellow pencil erasers, and our party, just beginning to get up, looked no larger than ants. Surely as high as we can go; the walls are too sheer. This must be what Tim brought us up here to see, and *here* is where God will speak to me. Again, I paused and listened intently in my spirit. But, there was no burning bush, no lightning bolt carving a special message on the craggy surfaces of the sheer mountain walls. No, not even a still, small voice. There was nothing but the sound of a gentle breeze, which seemed to be mocking me with hints of knowing whatever mysteries this place held.

I was drawn back out of my reverie as the group began to move on. And I had been wrong about not being able to go higher. Tim must have been half mountain goat! Our progress was slow, but it was still possible without having to resort to alpine scaling techniques. And then, without any warning, the rim loomed just ahead of us. As we peered over it, an incredible sight met our eyes! There, nestled at the base of even higher mountains, was a bowl-shaped meadow—a miniature green valley, with-rich, soft grass growing in abundant profusion. For four days, we had not seen grass anywhere, and now, here, in this hidden mountain fortress, was a little meadow no more than a football field in width and three in length. It beckoned us like an oasis in an arid desert.

Tim led us down through the center of it, and I marveled at the little wildflowers growing among the grass like bright baubles against green velvet, and cactus plants reaching skyward. It was a desert Eden, preserved intact in the hollow of God's hand, for, heaven only knew, how long. When we reached the far side of the valley, we started climbing again, up the side of the wall that enclosed the valley. But, we went only a short distance this time. We came to a rock ridge that created a six-foot parallel overhang which extended over the valley below. Around its perimeter was a man-made wall of stone, about four feet tall, making an enclosure that was around twelve feet long. At one end, in close proximity to where we stood, there was a little entry-way, possibly two feet square.

"What is that?" I asked, my voice having dropped almost to a whisper.

"An Indian granary," Tim replied. "We figure the Anazazi must have grown corn in that field and stored it up here. It was a well-concealed cache. We've been up here many times, but only recently discovered it. I doubt if more than two dozen white men have ever seen it."

I reached out and touched the ancient wall, thinking now, at last, God would give the revelation I had been so longing for and that would crown this wonderful trip. Perhaps some truth that had been eluding mankind for fifteen hundred years, Lord?

I held my breath, but there was nothing. And yet, at the same time, I sensed the Lord was trying to get me to see something. Frustrated, I joined the others as they filed back across the meadow. We descended quickly, because time had slipped by. We had a certain number of miles to go that day, and we had to get off on time to do them all in daylight. So down the side of the canyon we went, without resting, and my disposition went down with us.

Why hadn't God spoken?

I concentrated on the business of getting down. For some reason, the footing was trickier than going up. Every so often, someone would slide on the loose stones, sending a shower of small and not so small rocks down on those below. Each time it happened, the perpetrator would yell, "Rocks, rocks!" as we had been instructed to, and those below would then scramble to get out of the way.

I didn't know whether it irritated me more to have to dodge other people's rocks, or to have to warn others to dodge mine. By the time we reached the camp, my legs, which were not in shape for mountain climbing, were trembling in rebellion over the exertion I had required of them. The sun was already beating down and, to put it mildly, I was pooped.

"Okay, you climbers," Dee called, "I'm sorry, but you're going to have to get a move on. As you can see, everyone else is packed and ready to go. So grab what's left of breakfast and get your gear in the rafts."

Chewing on a piece of cold toast, I tried to stuff my sleeping pad into its watertight girdle. Of all the times to be cantankerous, it had to pick this one! And the more I stuffed and jammed, the more recalcitrant it became. It must have put on five pounds overnight!

At this opportune moment, one of the "sidewalk supervisors" made an astute observation: "Behold, an irresistible force suddenly meets the immovable object."

I said nothing. But, I fought an urge to fling the half-stuffed sleeping pad into the river . . . with my critic to speedily follow!

And that was the instant God finally chose to speak to me: *Merlin, that is it.*

"What is it?" I said half-aloud, even though I knew it was God.

That is what I want to speak to you about on this trip. And this is where I want to speak to you about it, down here where people live. They don't live on mountaintops, or in hidden meadows, or beside ancient relics. They live down here, where it is hot, and they are tired—and irritable. And down here is where people need to learn, and where you need to learn. And what I want you to learn is how not to be irritated in these everyday experiences of life.

I stood stock-still, oblivious to those around me, as the full impact of this hit me. I was so intently tuned in, that when I looked up, to my surprise, Bruce had packed my pad for me, and my gear as well, and was preparing to stow it in the raft. Saying nothing, I went over and climbed into the raft. God had spoken and now I was to begin learning by doing.

We were to encounter even bigger rapids that morning, with our rafts now lashed together, two and two. As we approached the rapids ahead, they sounded like Niagara Falls, with waves so steep, it seemed like we would surely be sucked down into them. And when we hit bottom, they towered so high above us, that looking up at them, it seemed like we would surely be swamped as they crashed in upon us. But, wonder of wonders, they didn't, and unbelievably, we would scoot up the other side, like a roller coaster racing towards the next breathtaking drop! Everyone was laughing and shouting, and, in between the rough stretches, we would bail for all we were worth, because each gallon we bailed out lightened the raft by eight pounds! We knew other "showers" lay just ahead of us and the better part of wisdom was not valor—but bailing.

In the midst of all this frantic activity, I had the uncanny feeling one might experience in the eye of a hurricane, as I meditated on what God had told me. Though I almost never let it show, irritability was still very much a part of my basic nature. And now God wanted to change that nature. I was nonplused—He proposed to change something that was at the very core of my being. Which meant that, by the grace of God, and with my full permission and cooperation, the Holy Spirit *could* change not only who I was, but *how* I was.

Certainly, it was scriptural: love is not irritable or resentful (1 Cor. 13:5 RSV). "Let me show you a more excellent way," surfaced in my awareness, and gradually I realized that God intended to work that irritability out of me. In His patience, He would take a lifetime to teach me, if a lifetime was needed. But, I saw, as I bailed, it didn't have to take that long. It could happen much sooner. It all depended on how badly I *wanted* to change.

The revelation was so exciting to me that my spirit soared to heavenly places for the rest of our trip! I enjoyed the last two days enormously, and the plane trip home went smoothly. But in my mind, I kept going back over the revelation God had given me during this time of rest. The Holy Spirit was able to work remarkable, even astounding, changes at the very core of who we are—*if* we believed that He would, and *if* we cooperated with Him to the fullest extent. Because this was the purpose for our time on earth: to be conformed more and more to the image of Jesus Christ. For me, right now, His target was irritability. For someone else, it might be jealousy; for another, self-righteousness, gluttony, lust.. . . I knew Jesus had promised to present us blameless before the Father. However, He did not promise the process would be painless.

And so, because a preacher invariably focuses on the sin area in which God has most recently been dealing with him personally, my first sermon back at Praise Center was on the subject of irritability. I shared it all, the fruit of my resting time. And then found that, as the old Pentecostals used to say, I "had to walk through the fire of my own preaching."

CHAPTER ELEVEN

We Can Change

I should have expected it, of course. The moment I preached on irritability, I began to see more clearly just how quickly it can flare up into anger, even violence. How it closes off lines of communication, grieves the Holy Spirit, and can ultimately destroy relationships. I should have anticipated that God would now permit me to see just how irritable I could become at heart.

It was far more than I suspected. The old saying, "There, but for the grace of God, go I," took on new meaning for me, as I experienced an avalanche of opportunities to be irritable. For one solid week after that sermon, it seemed that everything that happened, irritated me. I was shocked, not once, but repeatedly, at my core reaction to things.

But there was victory, too. Because each time that I was able to praise God for showing me who I was, I was able to reject the irritation that had tried to control me. And when I was tempted to give in, it became clear that I actually had a split-second choice.

I could choose to respond like Christ, or like Merlin.

It wasn't always that way. I was reminded of an ugly incident that I hadn't thought of in years. It was during World War II, and I was in an elegant night club, a cocky young paratrooper out on the town. The master of ceremonies had added to his sophisticated welcoming jokes a few comments on the paratrooper with his highly polished jump boots and silver wings. He asked me where I was stationed and how many jumps I had made, and then in a show of wartime partriotism announced, "Set the trooper up with the best drink in the house!"

There was applause, and I beamed in this well-deserved respect. Five minutes passed, and then ten, and still no drink. I began to realize that the emcee had just made a few cheap points at my expense, and my anger started to smoulder. By the time thirty minutes had passed, I was in a white-hot rage. I reached down and grabbed the leg of my chair, then I suddenly stood up and crashed the chair across the top of the table.

The music stopped, and all eyes turned in my direction, fear on many faces. In the hush that followed, I growled, "I want my drink! *Now!*" The waiter practically ran to bring it to me.

What I needed to see, in recalling that incident, was just who I was, without Christ. But it was also a testimony to just how much basic personality change God can work in a life, when we truly cooperate with Him. And I also had to see that there was still work that needed to be done, for even today I had to stand against being irritated when a waitress would forget to bring a cup of coffee. The point was, I could choose.

I thought, then, of Ben Trion. Ben could have chosen; indeed, he might have, had he set his heart on being conformed more to the image of Jesus Christ. Ben had an ideal childhood. He was bright and healthy, had loving parents, and received the best education available. His life was relatively carefree all the way through pre-med school, and his career in medicine couldn't have been more promising. Everyone in his family was proud to call him "theirs."

But Ben had one problem his parents had not been able to help. He had a temper. It was no more or less than thousands of young men just like him, and probably a good deal less than mine had been that night in the night club. In stress, he reacted just as any other human being might; in fact, as each of us might, given the same circumstances, unless we have had a powerful change worked in our personalities.

One afternoon, Ben was driving on a busy, one-way metropolitan street. Cars were parked on both sides of the street, so that there was only room for one lane of traffic. Ben was in no particular hurry, but the guy in the sports car behind him was. When Ben failed to leave the light the instant it turned green, he started honking.

Ben responded with typical carefree laughter. A little thing like that wasn't going to bother him. But, of course, underneath, it did. And when he did start to move, he went just a little more slowly than he might have otherwise.

The other driver, seeing Ben laughing, became even more irritated. Since it was obvious that Ben was not making any effort to keep the traffic moving, he gently nudged the back of Ben's car with his front bumper. Now Ben was getting angry. Though he did move out a little faster after the next light, by the time he got to the third light, he was furious. Who did that guy think he was, bumping into his car that way? He'd better not try that stunt again!

And then, just to show him that he was not about to be intimidated, he deliberately did not start right up when the light turned green. The driver behind him gave his car a stronger nudge this time. And now Ben exploded. He drove forward about ten feet, then suddenly stopped and jammed his car into reverse, ramming his antagonist's little car at full speed.

After the crash, Ben shifted into low and drove off, noting in the rear-view mirror that the car behind him hadn't moved. Well, that will give him something to think about for a while, he thought.

Several hours later, Ben was back in his comfortable home, still chuckling about that jerk who had tried to push him out of the way. The door bell rang, and there was a policeman, who asked if he was the driver of a blue Ford with a certain license number.

"Yes, why?"

"Were you driving it this afternoon at 2:00 P.M.?"

"Yes, officer," he said, smiling. "Did that guy file a complaint against me?"

"No, he didn't. He's dead. It is my duty to warn you that anything you say may be used against you. You are under arrest."

A freak incident? Perhaps. But the potential had been living inside Ben since the day he was born. As it is in each of us, until we give Christ permission to do something about it.

I had given Him that permission, and now I had preached about it, and what a week I went through afterwards! But it was also an indication that I was onto something very significant. This whole business of letting the Holy Spirit change us—of seeing there were areas where God wanted us to be changed and then giving Him permission to do a deep, perhaps even painful, work in us—really wasn't much in fashion these days. And I suspected that the reason it was no longer being preached the way it had been up until a couple of generations ago, was akin to what I had just experienced. If I was going to preach on the sin of anger, then I had better be prepared for Him to deal with my own anger at a far deeper level than I had previously wanted to look at!

And yet, if anything concrete had come out of my wilderness sabbatical in the way of fresh revelation (other than my own need to stay absolutely centered in Christ, and His peace), it was this. So, two weeks later, I preached on it again. My subject: Believe that the Holy Spirit *can* change you, and He *will* change you.

I told our congregation, "My flesh does not want to speak at Praise Center, because whenever I preach something that really strikes home, it seems that Satan always throws a spiritual wrench at me!" We laughed, as I told them of the unbelievably irritating week I had just had after my previous sermon. Again I emphasized that irritation is a tool of Satan to destroy our body, our harmony with others, our witness for Christ and even our fellowship with God the Father. I thought no more about it . . . until the following morning.

I had asked my son Bruce to climb up in one of the avocado trees in our back yard and trim off a couple of the top branches. Without complaining, he got up bright and early, and, saw in hand, proceeded to climb to the top of the tree to carry out my request. I waited at the base of the tree, but the limb was so high up that I went in the house and upstairs to the outside balcony in order to see where he should make the cut. One limb came off with no problem. Just as he was reaching for the second, I realized that he was in danger. I shouted in alarm, "Bruce, don't—"

But it was too late! Suddenly his body left the tree and he was crashing to the ground twenty-five feet below. I felt sick as I heard the awful thud of his body smashing into the solid earth. And I heard a horrible groan. . . .

As I ran downstairs I remembered where I had heard that same kind of a groan before—from dying men in Vietnam field hospitals.

"Oh, God, oh, God" was all I could say as I ran, and for some reason, I recalled what I had said in church—was Satan trying to take my son? "Oh, God!"

As I ran to Bruce, I could hear his groans, and thoughts of a broken back or neck raced through my brain. When I reached him he could hardly breathe. With some relief I realized he was conscious. After I was able to get him into the house and on his bed, he was still groaning in intense pain. I called the doctor and then rushed him to the hospital. As we sped along I kept thanking the Lord and by faith believing He could use even this for good. The praise became spontaneous, when the x-rays revealed that although there were multiple fractures of vertabrae along the spine, the spine itself showed no evidence of damage. Hallelujah!

In four short weeks after the accident Bruce was already coming into the office in the mornings; in fact we had a hard time keeping him down. It is with a real sense of praise that I realize God continues to strengthen him daily.

As I reflected later on the accident, there was much indeed to praise God for. Bruce had landed on perfectly flat soil—no rocks or hard places or depressions anywhere. Moreover, it was soil that only the previous week we had started watering twice as much as before, so that instead of being hard and dry as it had been, it was moist and springy to the touch. And then, there was his landing position—had he landed on his neck or his pelvis, or stretched out an arm to break his fall, or had he come straight down on his heels with his knees stiff (the worst position a paratrooper could land in). . . . No. A loving God had protected him, and it wasn't hard to imagine angels swooping down and breaking the worst of the fall, and making sure that he landed perfectly flat, thus spreading the impact over the maximum possible area.

I prayed then, and asked the Holy Spirit if there was anything else I needed to see about what had happened. What came to me next was a surprise. Two years earlier, I had shared with the congregation my growing hunger that they all be delivered from immoral thoughts and actions. We had had some instances of immorality over at North County, that had caught us completely off guard—caught *me* off guard, I should say. I had naively assumed that any Christian who had given his life to the Lord and was trying to live for Him and walk with Him, simply wouldn't be committing immoral acts. So I had hit the subject hard, pointing out that we were accountable before God for the cleanliness of our temples, and that uncleanness invariably began in the mind. It was about time we rolled up our sleeves and started doing some spiritual warfare. And we could begin by taking command over what went on in our minds. Harassing thoughts might come to us, but we could refuse them.

"Bringing into captivity every thought" Paul had written the believers in 2 Corinthians 10:5, and I felt he really meant it.

The day after that sermon, I had flown to Indiana for a crusade, and one of my hosts was showing me an exhaust fan that he had installed in his barn, to cool it. When he switched the fan on, the entire remains of a rat were blown in my face, and at that moment my spiritual ears very clearly discerned an evil laugh. But neither my host nor his friend were laughing; on the contrary, they were horrified and did their best to clean me up. It was an eerie incident, but I had thought no more about it—until now.

Less than a year ago, I had preached again on the subject of pure thoughts, this time emphasizing the need for us to let the Holy Spirit do a cleansing and purifying work within us, particularly in the area of our minds. For it was what proceeded *out* of a man's heart that defiled him, and the Holy Spirit *could* purify a man's heart. What was more, God was calling us—both as a body and as individuals—to entertain *only* pure thoughts. With His help, we could be freed from any desire to even think or want immoral things. We could live in the power of His Word: "Whatsoever things are pure . . . Think on these things."

A few hours later, I was at home, walking in our little avocado grove, when I was suddenly struck from behind on the leg. I collapsed in great pain; it felt as though someone had thrown a baseball at me from very close range and it hit with tremendous impact. I heard someone laugh snidely quite near, and I wrenched around, as I lay on the ground, to see who had thrown it.

There was no one else in the grove. Nor could I find a baseball or a rock or any projectile which could have hit me. The doctor had no explanation, beyond the fact that something had to have caused it. It could not have happened, if I were merely walking along, as I had told him. The outcome was real enough! I was on crutches for five months.

Now, as I prayed about this thing that had happened to Bruce, right after I had preached on believing that the Holy Spirit could change our basic natures, suddenly these other "coincidences" came to mind. It began to look like someone didn't want me preaching about inner sin and the crucial need to change, and that indeed profound change *was* possible. That someone was Satan.

Why was it such a threat to him? There was nothing new about the message. . . . Except that you heard so little about it these days. Most of us probably wouldn't put the need for soul-searching change very high on our list of spiritual priorities. It is much easier to assume that we are unchangeable—"Well, that's just the way I am." After all don't we drive around with bumper stickers on our cars which proclaim to everyone—"Christians aren't perfect—just forgiven." Yes, God does love us just as we are but He loves us too much to leave us where we are.

Another very convenient alternative to the difficult and often painful process of changing is to simply blame our sins on the devil. How infinitely easier to just cast out a "demon of irritability"—magic-wand Christianity in keeping with our NOW generation with its easy answers. Buy now and pay later with instant credit and easy-time payments. The crunch comes later—with interest.

No, sin was sin, and that's all there was to it. The age-old battle between flesh and spirit would continue until Jesus returned. As Paul himself confessed, we would be faced with the choice of doing the things we knew we shouldn't, and not doing the things we knew we should. However, we could follow his example and do as he did, doing battle with self daily, even to the point of bringing every thought captive to Christ, waging all-out war against our sinful natures.

And we could be changed, as Paul was changed. In fact, it was God's purpose that we be changed continually into the image of His Son. I had seen people who had fought the good fight with all their might and had gained real victory. They truly *were* changed! And since my present assignment was irritability, I was going to go on battling against it, until I was an overcomer. And then, the Lord would have another assignment. How did the old hymn go?

"To him that overcometh the crown of life shall be. He with the King of Glory shall reign eternally!"

Changing—deep down changing—that was what real righteousness was all about. "Blessed are they which hunger and thirst after righteousness," Jesus had said on the mount, *for they shall be filled.* There was the promise; it was about time we did some hungering and thirsting. So I would go on preaching about the need for us to change—no matter what Satan did. Only now, I would make a point of asking our people to pray for their pastors, and especially, for the Lord to protect their households.

CHAPTER TWELVE

A Grateful Heart

During a recent Missionary Sunday at Praise Center, Marilyn Wyman came forward to share a little of what was happening at the foundation.

"Do you remember us telling you about the man in Norway who had such a burden for Liberia? For years, he had been praying for the Lord to create an opening for the Holy Spirit there and he believed it would happen! Methodist Bishop Bennie Warner and Vice President, Dr. William Tolbert, Jr., of Liberia were both sympathetic; all that was needed was the right vehicle. As he read *Prison to Praise*, the Lord witnessed to him that this was it. So he contacted us. To demonstrate his own commitment, he sent five hundred dollars toward the project."

She looked up and smiled, and everyone smiled back, in anticipation.

"Well, we've prayed much about it, and yesterday we wrote to let him know that we will be sending ten thousand copies of *Prison to Praise!*"

The announcement was greeted with resounding

applause as the people signaled their delighted surprise.

"Of course," Marilyn added, "we first have to pay for the ten thousand copies to be printed." And there was general laughter. "But we are praising God for what He is going to do in Liberia, through one small book called *Prison to Praise*. Think of it. The evangelism of a whole country!"

She paused and looked out over the congregation before going on.

"I have one other little matter to share with you; it has to do with the mailing list." This was greeted with groans of dismay as memories of our computer disaster came to many minds. "No, not *that* mailing list, thank heaven! We need to update our list of correspondents. As you know, through the foundation, some twenty-five hundred Christians across America have volunteered to correspond with inmates in prisons all over the world. Many times, it's the only Christian contact these prisoners will ever have, and we've had some wonderful praise reports of men and women who have accepted Christ and had their lives changed, thanks to the ministry of these correspondents who are known as our 'team writers.'"

As Marilyn went on, my mind drifted back to one such example which had crossed my desk just the week before. The team writer, "Aunt Harriet," was a local woman, who had been an elderly, retired psychiatric worker when Roy had first called on her in the hospital. All he did was talk about God loving her and she considered herself a rather staunch atheist. She was doubly bitter, having just lost a beloved nephew to leukemia, and when Roy suggested that Jesus could heal the pain and bitterness in her heart, her response was: "Prove it." So Roy prayed for her, and after he left the room, that's just what happened. The Lord came to her, and did indeed prove it. Now Aunt Harriet, age seventy-six, has been writing a number of prisoners for some time, telling them about the unsuspected love of God for them. What I specifically recalled was an answer she had just received from a young man in prison in Nigeria, who had been sentenced to death and was awaiting execution. He shared in his own inimitable style:

Dear Aunt Harriet:

It has happened, it has happened, it has happened! Praise God, hallelujah! Listen to me: God has heard your fervent and faithful prayers for my critical, bereaved opportunities. You knew I was a condemned-to-death boy for an offense which I never committed, but God has delivered me in the court of appeal. I am a free man today, not even to serve one day of my sentence, praise God. . . . I insisted always in praying to God that I am no thief or robber, and therefore I let Him plead my cause. Then I wrote to Merlin Carothers, who transferred my letter to you. You prayed earnestly that God would save me, and now He has. May God almighty prolong your life, for my sake!

As Marilyn concluded her appeal, she shared the following. "So what we need are some volunteers to come down and go through our files of team writers to bring our address list up to date. It will only take a few people a few days, and don't worry; we won't burn you out on the first day."

Then Jim Dilley, one of our elders, got up to make another announcement that had an important bearing on our outreach. "You all know that we have been looking forward to that day when the Lord would bring people here from all over the country, and even the world, to learn how to go about putting praise to work in their daily lives. You remember, Merlin told you that one day people would even be coming to live in some of our homes for a season? Well, that day has arrived a little sooner than we thought. But that's often the way it is, with God. It seems that the first contingent, some twenty people from South Africa, will be arriving on the 21st of this month. They'll be coming here to live with us and share with us, for about three days. We are going to put them up in various homes, so pray, and if you feel the Holy Spirit's leading, sign up on the bulletin board, when you leave. Then the pastors will go over the sign-up sheet, and will make the assignments, accordingly."

I grinned, listening to Jim; for once, God's timetable was ahead of mine. I thought of all the other things that He had recently shown me that He would one day be doing—the mountain and the new church and retreat center and . . . would they too come to pass sooner than I dared hope? But now was not the time for wishful thinking; now was the time to enter in. God would be working out our tomorrows as long as we flowed with His todays.

It was good to be back at Praise Center and a part of things again. It was good to sing, "He Is Lord" with all our friends, and enjoy the subtle harmonies of our singing group, The Joyful Praise. And it was especially good to see spontaneous praise welling up from so many grateful hearts. Over to the left, a group of deaf people were following the service through sign language of a volunteer translator. If *they* could be grateful. . . .

Seated up on the platform with the other pastors and elders, I found that praise welling up in me again, too. God had been so unbelievably good to us, during our "trek in the wilderness." From the park, He had led us to Central High School, and from there to Miller High School. We have now been there for more than a year. A beautiful school, complete with an air-conditioned auditorium. It's full and overflowing every Sunday. We know that if it would hold four times as many it would still be packed, even though our school building is nearly impossible for visitors to find. (If you are ever near Escondido, I would like to extend an invitation for you to come and worship with us. But, please, call the foundation office during the week for directions—619-741-2755.)

I thought again of how good it would be, when we finally had our own church, our permanent home in the promised land, as it were. But before I could finish the thought, I was praising God for the unifying work He had done in our body, during this wilderness time. For it had been a time of sifting; God had used our common adversity to winnow out those who weren't willing to meet in a park or a school, or take on the extra responsibilities that we were now requiring of our members. "When the going gets tough, the tough get going," took on a paradoxical meaning. When the going got tough, the tough stayed . . . and stood together . . . and waited on the Lord. I sensed that during all we had gone through together, God was building for the future. For no matter where we met or what our numbers were, we had become a church.

I smiled to myself, as another thought came to me. Obviously Praise Center had gotten along very well without me, which was a good lesson for me to learn. I had been laboring under a burden of "indispensability" and it was good to be rid of it. Attendance had remained steady, and even increased.

The same thing was true of the foundation, I

discovered, as I started going back into the office. I noticed how well the staff was flowing in the Spirit together; there was laughter, with good-natured kidding and a feeling of quiet peace about the place—that, I had to admit, had not been there before. There were still problems, of course, like the one with our team writers' list that Marilyn had just shared, but you got the feeling that God was very much in control of the situation.

Did it mean that the place was better off without me? No, hardly that. But it did mean that when I was there, I had better be a source of peace myself, well-centered in my trust that God was in charge, instead of broadcasting anxiety and striving in my own strength. As the leader, I was called to set the example of abiding in His peace.

Other good things were emerging as a result of my sabbatical. I received a call from Trinity Broadcasting. "We think it's fine, Merlin, that you took enough time off to get truly renewed. But it's been three months now; aren't you about renewed up?"

"Well, it does seem like God is beginning to re-involve me in all phases of the ministry," I could truthfully reply.

"Good! How soon can you come back and start taping another 65 shows for us? Because we need to get our fall schedule lined up." And I told them I would let them know soon.

And then the Lord took care of another concern

that had been in the back of my mind for some time. Ever since the North County affair, I had sensed an aloofness among some of the evangelical pastors in the local area. I had hoped it would dissipate with time, but two years had passed, and it hadn't. This became clear a few months ago, when I had written a personal letter to each of nine pastors in San Diego, enlisting their aid and support in our endeavor to get books into the county jail there. Not one of them had responded, or even replied.

And about that same time, an article appeared in the *San Diego Union*, quoting a local pastor as saying I had questionable ethics. At the time the article was printed, I had been more than just irritated and was ready to confront the pastor who had given the quote and demand an explanation and a retraction. But the Lord strongly checked me, and once again I had remained silent.

Then I had pretty much forgotten it, until, out of the blue, the Holy Spirit last week suddenly seemed to say: ask Roy to set up lunch with this particular pastor, and have fellowship with him. So it was arranged. The pastor and his wife came, and had lunch with Roy and Marilyn and me, and we had a wonderful time of fellowship. When we sat down, I sensed that the pastor was a little uptight about the quote in the article, so I brought it up rather than keep him hanging. I asked him if he could give me an example of what he had meant by "questionable ethics on my part."

He thought for a moment and said, "I was at a meeting of local San Diego pastors, and the subject of your letter came up. You were asking our help in placing and paying for free books to go into the county jail. As it happened, every one of us had tried at one time or another to get books into that jail, and it was just an impossibility. We had individually and as a ministerial group representing all our churches, been unable to get any county official to help us in any way. Since you were asking our help to do something that we knew could not be done, the consensus of opinion was that there had to be something not quite right about your kind of ministry. And if it was not right locally, it stood to reason that it couldn't be right nationally."

"But it's not impossible," I smiled. "We've done it. We've placed more than two thousand books in that jail."

"You have? I don't believe it! *How?*"

"God has called the Foundation of Praise specifically to distribute books to prisons and deprived areas," I explained, hoping that I wasn't coming across proud, "and it is He who arranges the coincidences and opens the doors. He always seems to find a way."

"Okay," our friend said, "but you still haven't told me how."

"Did you know the chaplain had a brother?"

He paused. "Yes, he's a doctor, isn't he?"

I nodded. "It turns out that he's also a committed

Christian. The Lord brought him into contact with us for a specific reason—" and I stopped as I saw him putting the pieces together.

"So. . . ."

I nodded again.

Our friend just shook his head. "Merlin, I am so sorry. Look, I'll do anything you want me to, anything to make up for. . . ."

I smiled. "I don't want you to do anything. But I'm awfully glad we got all that cleared up! And before the main course too!"

"So am I!" he breathed a sigh of relief.

The waitress was just heading our way with lunch. Throughout the rest of our time together, the unity of His Spirit drew us closer and I realized then an "unseen guest" was sharing our table.

But by no means were all of the local pastors aloof; in fact, an extraordinary incident involving one of them some months ago led to a most exciting miracle of physical healing. I include it here, because, somehow, in a way I don't fully understand, it has something to do with the whole new thing that God is on the verge of doing with Praise Center and the foundation.

"Many wonders and signs were done" say the Scriptures in Acts 2:43, and, indeed, the Lord often puts His seal on a work or a teaching, by following it with miracles, much like an artist putting his signature in the corner of a finished canvas. But God will also announce, by means of miracles, that He is raising up a new work or ministry or prophet, as if to say, "Look. Come and see. This is of me, and is under my hand and anointing." When the Carpenter first started to preach, it was the miracles that brought the people, though it was the truth that kept and held them.

At Praise Center and the Foundation of Praise, we are tremendously encouraged because of the sudden burst of miracles that have begun to happen. Nearly every Sunday there is at least one report of an amazing answer to prayer. But to return to our story. To protect their privacy, I'll call them Bill and Betty Walker.

Early in March, the foundation received a call from Betty. She and her husband, Bill, were not members of Praise Center, but Betty had a favor to ask: Would I come to the hospital and pray for Bill who was a terminal cancer patient there. Roy, who took the call, informed her that I was away at the moment, taping a television show, and was under a great deal of pressure at the time—could he possibly help? And so she explained, haltingly, why she had called, starting at the beginning.

Her mother had been attending Praise Center and had urged Betty to read *Prison to Praise*. Betty had always resented her mother when she got on her "charismatic kick," but finally she read the book. For the first time, it dawned on her that there was more to Christianity than she had ever dreamed possible, and a few months later, she became a charismatic

Christian herself. A short time thereafter, her husband, Bill, began to feel sort of washed-out, run down. He had been a heavy smoker all his life, but finally, in December of '77, he was coughing so badly, he quit. But his cough did not. It continued, especially when he tried to get to sleep, just as it had for twenty years.

By February, Bill felt so exhausted he could barely drag himself to work. On February 23, during one violent coughing spell, he started coughing up blood, and had a severe pain in his chest. His first thoughts were "heart attack." He was in no frame of mind to continue working that day and he went home. Betty called their family doctor, who told her to bring him right in. The doctor arranged for x-rays and, though Bill didn't know it, the x-ray revealed a tumor on his lung the size of a grapefruit.

He was admitted to Palomar Hospital on February 28, and they began a complete series of tests—liver scan, bone scan, lymph glands. These were all okay, so they scheduled an operation to remove the tumor on March 7, informing Betty that it would take about five and one-half hours. When, at the end of two and one-half hours, they wheeled him out, Betty knew that something was terribly wrong. The surgeon confirmed her worst fears, telling her that when they had opened Bill up, they found that the tumor was malignant and had wound around the main aorta of the heart, around the bronchial tubes, around the back of the heart like tentacles, and had even attached itself to the back wall of the chest. There was no way that they could get it all; if they tried, the operation would kill him. It was beyond surgery now. There was only one thing to do. Leave it in there, and sew him back up. The surgeon said that if they started cobalt treatments, they might be able to slow any further spreading, but that was about all that could be hoped for. He gave Bill thirty days to live.

As soon as she could get herself together, Betty prayed an amazing prayer. "Lord, I accept this as a fact. Now you turn it into a blessing and do something that will glorify you." She left the hospital with unusual peace. Each day her faith increased.

That afternoon, the pastor from their church came to see Bill. He prayed for Bill and, in the course of his prayer, he said something that seemed completely irrelevant—"and Lord, bless Merlin Carothers' ministry"—and continued on with his prayer as if nothing had happened. But it struck Betty as so odd that she decided to call the foundation and ask if I could come and pray for her husband.

Roy told her that he would check with me and get back to her, and the next morning, when he reported all this, I said that of course we would go. And when we got to the hospital that afternoon, we met Bill's pastor in the hallway. I explained to him Betty's request and asked if it was all right. He said, "Of course." He was happy for any hope we could share with Bill.

Bill was conscious when we came in, but he was

gray-looking as he lay on the bed. There was a tube up his nose and another in his arm, as well as one coming out of his back. His eyes followed us, but they were lackluster and barely open. "Would you like us to pray for you?"

"Yes," he whispered.

We had brought some oil with us, and with this Roy anointed him. Then we laid on hands, Betty joining us. It was apparent that he was in much pain. "Father," I prayed, "we hold your son Bill up to you. You made him, Father, and to you he will return. We pray that you would not call him now, but heal the cancer that is within him. Touch him, Lord, with your healing power, and restore him to perfect wholeness. Make him completely whole, that he might live to your glory and to magnify your name. All this we ask in the name of your Son, Jesus."

Bill did not say or do anything; I was not aware of any heat or other sensation indicative of something having happened. We smiled and said goodbye to Betty, and left.

The next day, Betty called Roy and thanked him again, reporting incidentally that Bill seemed to feel a little better. Three days later, she called again to say that Bill had been released from the intensive care unit, and was able to sit up in bed and read. He was reading *Prison to Praise*.

The next time Betty called, it was with the report that Bill had started thanking God for his doctors, for all the equipment they had and the tools they used.

One evening, he concentrated on praising God for his hacking cough and said, "Lord, I turn this all over to you. I believe you want to heal me." He stopped coughing immediately. For the first time in twenty years, he went to sleep without coughing. He never experienced those terrible hacking spasms of coughing again.

The surgeon was still convinced that death was imminent. But, since Bill seemed to be feeling better, on March 14, he took the stitches out and said that he could go home. He didn't tell Bill, but he thought that he might as well live out what little time he had left in familiar surroundings. So Bill went home. And continued to praise God. And continued to feel better. In fact, by April 7, he felt strong enough that he wanted to do some work around the house and mow the lawn. Betty was having a hard time keeping him quiet. She called the surgeon and pleaded to bring Bill in for another x-ray. The surgeon reluctantly agreed.

When he and the radiologist looked at the x-ray, they were astonished. "It's smaller!" one said aloud, and indeed, it had shrunken from the size of a grapefruit to the size of an orange. But now there was another mass below his rib cage, and the surgeon could not keep the hopelessness from his voice. He prescribed more cobalt treatments, and would not change his prognosis, despite the shrinkage of the main tumor.

Bill, however, appeared to continue improving,

gaining weight and strength with every passing day. Finally, when he was really growing impatient at having to stay home, and talked continually about going back to work, Betty arranged for another series of x-rays, and on April 22, he was x-rayed again. When the developed x-rays came to the surgeon's office, the usually taciturn surgeon was astounded. "Look at these x-rays!" he exclaimed. "They are clear! Even the mass below your rib cage is gone! I don't believe this!"

Even so, he would not admit that it was a miracle of divine intervention, but he did say that he had never read or heard of cobalt treatments having that kind of effect on cancer in such an advanced state.

Bill and Betty have just returned from what amounts to a second honeymoon with the Lord. They went to visit relatives, to witness to them, and then took their camper on a tour of national parks, where they witnessed to hundreds of people about the marvelous healing power of God. They are both praising God all the time now, and their lives have become a daily adventure with Christ!

As I spoke with Bill this morning, checking out the details of his story, he said, "I haven't felt this good in thirty years! I want to work for God. I'll do whatever He wants me to do, because I wouldn't even have a life if He hadn't given it back to me. If He wants me to work . . . fine. If He wants to take me to heaven, that will be even finer."

And so, we wait upon the Lord with a sense of

expectation, to see what is to come next. The people of Praise Center would be content to go on meeting in loaned school auditoriums indefinitely, but the local laws are stringent on that: we can use school facilities only temporarily, and must demonstrate that progress is being made towards a permanent facility of our own.

Here was one more thing for me to get uptight over, but praise God, I was not giving in to the temptation. I knew He was in charge and was working out His plan.

CHAPTER THIRTEEN

Mount Pisgah

There's a young man in our church by the name of Ford Silsby, whose story I told in detail in *Bringing Heaven Into Hell*. Little did I know he would figure prominently in God's latest development for the people of Praise Center.

Ford was born with good looks. Strong and tall, in high school he excelled in several sports—football, wrestling, and swimming. Blessed with the sort of looks and personality that made him extremely popular, life seemed to give him everything he wanted, and he took all that he could get. As he himself put it, "I used to wake up every morning, wondering what I could do to make myself enjoy the day more."

One night, or rather early morning, on his way home from an all-night party, his small convertible veered off the road, and plunged over a three hundred foot embankment. When they finally found him, Ford's skull was split open, and his brain stem was severely damaged. The doctors said that if he ever came out of the coma, he would almost certainly be a vegetable for the rest of his life.

But his parents and Christian friends began a prayer battle for him and stuck with it for weeks, despite all the negative reports, and Ford was literally snatched from death to life. He regained consciousness but had lost his memory, his learned skills and most of his motor coordination. But he was not a vegetable, and he was determined to be rehabilitated.

His first faltering steps on the road to recovery were pathetic. The coaches of the teams he had once starred on took pity on him and let him work out with the teams in the practices, but all his skill, coordination and stamina were gone. In football, he had lost his agility, in swimming his endurance, and wrestlers much smaller than he could throw him at will. Worst of all, his old worldly buddies now mocked him, or reacted with condescending pity. Although these were painful experiences, they were part of God's plan. When former friendships proved fallible, Ford turned to the only source of strength and comfort which would be sufficient for the long road ahead. Jesus became his friend, his coach and his strength. The rest is history, astounding in its scope. Ford improved to the point where he won a football scholarship to college and today he is playing football and helping other young boys see that real life is giving, not getting.

One evening, about a year and a half ago, this

remarkable young man was out jogging, as part of his program to get back into top physical shape. He was running along Route 78, going east out of Escondido, when on an impulse, he turned in on an old road and decided to jog up to the top of a little mountain that is a local landmark on the outskirts of town. (We use the term "mountain" euphemistically in these parts. A sort of petering out of the Sierra Madres; if real mountains were coughs, these would be hiccups.)

What made this particular mountain a landmark was that in 1929, a local entrepreneur named Andrew Houghtelin bought it and intended to build an inn at the top. By way of preparation, he spent $50,000, an enormous amount in those days, grading a road and pouring three concrete platform foundations, including one at the summit. On this one, he erected a hundred foot, wood and stucco replica of a Plains Indian tepee, in honor of his wife, who was an Indian. Planning to incorporate it into the design of his inn, his dreams collapsed in the Crash of '29. Further financing was impossible to raise, and when his wife died tragically, he left the tepee standing, as sort of a memorial to her.

Through the years, the tepee remained the most prominent landmark in the area, visible for fifty miles atop its lofty perch. For forty years, planes used it as a visual orientation point, on their approach to Mira Mar Naval Air Station; and because, for some inexplicable reason, the mountain was almost totally free of magnetic disturbance, unlike any of the others around it, it was periodically used to test sophisticated new radio equipment.

In recent years, the tepee itself had fallen on hard times. The stucco which had originally covered it had long since weathered off, and its old boards were beginning to rot and fall away. Its present owner, Andrew's son, Clair, had no inclination to refurbish it. Yet, from a distance, it still looked imposing, and the whole town had an affectionate place in their hearts for it, as it had been there before many of them were born.

This was the mountain that Ford jogged up, in the half light that hung over Escondido just after sunset. Later the following night, he jogged to our house, quite excited, to tell Mary and I what happened next. "I know this sounds crazy, but when I got to the top and looked around, the view was so beautiful, it almost took my breath away. And as I stood there, I felt God's presence, all around me. He seemed to be giving me a vision, that had to do with spreading the message of praise around the world." He paused and looked at me. "Pastor Carothers, I got an impression of buildings, and it seemed like He was saying that up here—this is where the headquarters of praise should be—not down in some hidden valley, or on a plain, but up here, on the top of this mountain."

I listened carefully to what Ford was saying, especially in light of the amazing work that God had done in his life, but when he finished, I simply could not respond with the enthusiasm he was hoping for.

"Well, that's very interesting," I said, "and—"

"Pastor Carothers, I believe we're supposed to claim that mountain for the Praise ministry!"

"Yes, but we don't even know if its's available."

"Oh, but it is. I checked on it today. The whole mountain is on a single forty-five acre lot."

And with that, I put the entire thing out of my mind. Land in these parts was going for $12,000 an acre, minimum.

But Ford was not to be discouraged. In ensuing days, he continued his investigation, and he discovered that while many real estate developers had been interested in the property—one for a resort hotel, another for a country club, and several others simply because it was prime land and ideal for the luxury retirement homes that were springing up around Escondido. But there were three things which discouraged them. First there was a clause in the deed which stipulated that alcoholic beverages could never be sold on that land. Secondly, the soil composition was such that it could never support the leach lines that would be necessary for sewage disposal. And thirdly, the land had been tied up in litigation for years, which made the first two points academic.

Except—Ford, steadfastly proceeding with what he was sure was the Lord's leading, went to see the owner and learned that the property had just come out of litigation and was about to go on the market. He urged me to go and talk to the owner, but still, I could not see it. So Ford turned to his father, Sandy Silsby, who is one of our elders, and Sandy talked to the other elders. Finally they all came to me and said, "Merlin, this just may be of the Lord, and if it is, we don't want to miss Him. It wouldn't do any harm for you to go and see this man."

And so I went. There were forty-five acres, all right, and if we took them all, he was willing to give them to us for $9,000 an acre, which, for suburban Escondido, was a real bargain. At that time, however, Praise Center didn't have $9,000—period. But Ford had said that the Lord would provide, and so I told the owner that I would be back.

In the meantime, I tried to persuade the elders that further speculation was fruitless, because of the soil composition. But our elders were not so easily discouraged. One of them had heard of a radical new design in leach systems which had just been developed for soil like ours. Though not yet in use in our area, it had been successfully tested elsewhere, and he had a hunch it just might work here.

"Well, Lord," I thought, "I guess I have to face the fact that I really don't want to be involved with building another church.

"Maybe there's still some hurt that hasn't healed, or subconsciously I'm afraid of getting hurt again. But even if this is so, I just don't see how we're ever going to raise that kind of money. Still, if you really are in this, then please change my heart, because the last thing I want to do is stand in the way of your will."

Thus it was, that when Roy called one afternoon, to see if we could all meet at the base of the mountain after work, I was able to muster at least partial enthusiasm. Not so, the others, who were genuinely excited, as we gathered just before sundown. The road up the mountain had long been washed out, so we would have to walk up. And up we went, winding back and forth above the old orange grove that covered the base and lower slopes of the mountain. At the first circular concrete foundation, we paused and looked to the east. Ford was right: the view was breathtaking. It seemed like a magnificent panoramic picture—too beautiful to be real, with groves and hills and vales receding into the distance. There was a wide valley beyond, and still farther a perimeter of mountains, taller and grander than the one we were standing on. All of which was bathed in the golden light of the last rays of the setting sun.

No one spoke. We were all trying to assimilate the majesty of what our eyes were taking in, and it was simply more than one could absorb in one sitting. It was the sort of place you wanted to come back to more than once. (And the eastern view continues to have that effect on everyone who sees it for the first time.) Finally, someone suggested that we had better move on, because we didn't have much daylight left.

We climbed higher, and came to the second concrete foundation, this one facing west. On a clear day, Ford had said, you could see the Pacific Ocean, thirty miles away. This evening the horizon was hazy, however; the sun was like an orange ball, hanging just above the western mountains. Those mountains, and all the vales and foothills in between, were shrouded with haze—the mountains themselves forming purple silhouettes, so still and beautiful in the haze that they looked unreal.

The whole horizon took on a mystical quality, like the setting for some mythical Shangri-la. Here, too, were little groves, tucked away at the foot of mountains, and some of the luxury homes that marked the outskirts of Escondido, the town itself being hidden behind the nearest foothills. Perhaps the name Escondido was born as the first settlers looked down into the valley below, for Escondido, most appropriately, means "beautiful hidden valley." As we watched, the sun began to disappear behind the mountains, its final rays reaching out to softly touch the mountain tops before retiring for the night. Down below, it was already dusk, and one by one the lights of the houses began to blink on here and there, then the street lights. Night had fallen.

"Come on, you guys," Roy called, and we moved on up the last short rise to the mountain's summit. From here, you could take in a 360 degree panorama. The sun was setting, and shades of night were fast creeping up the sides of the mountain. But still we stood there, without comment. There was no longer any question in my mind that God had brought us here, and that He did have some very special plan for this particular mountain, a plan that involved all of us standing there. I wondered if Moses had felt something like this, after all that time in the wilderness, when the Lord had taken him to the top of Mount Pisgah and shown him the promised land.

And looking around, I saw that everyone else was feeling the awesomeness of the moment. It was getting dark quickly now, and we realized that we should be heading down the mountain. But no one wanted to leave; no one even wanted to speak.

Finally, one of the men suggested that it was time we prayed and claimed the whole mountain for the Lord. So we joined hands and did just that. And as each of us prayed whatever the Lord had laid upon our hearts, someone said, "And Lord, you will have to find some solution for this tepee, because everyone around here has such a reverence for it, that they'd never let us take it down." With that prayer, we laughed, and started making our way down the mountain.

After that evening, every obstacle I had foreseen seemed to crumble and the pieces began to fit into place, as if manipulated by an unseen hand. Fortunately, among our elders we numbered some very sound businessmen, and they, along with the owner of the property, worked out a feasible plan for its purchase. The sums were high, but not impossible. Not if God was in it. We could no longer doubt that He was.

Concerning the leach system, a clause was written

into the agreement which said that if we could not obtain county approval for this system, the purchase would be annulled, and property and down payments would revert to the respective parties. As it turned out, the county did not approve of the system we proposed, but it did accept one very similar to it, and that hurdle was passed with no problem.

As we now looked to the Lord, He did bring in enough money for the first two down payments—just enough, and just in time. We were like a small plane struggling over a large mountain range, gaining just enough altitude to clear one peak, and then gaining the needed altitude to clear the next higher one looming just ahead. This was a pretty hairy way to "fly." We were learning the meaning of "coming in on a wing and a prayer."

One last hurdle to deal with even if we got the land: how could we ever afford to build? The answer was not long in coming: take a poll of the building skills that already exist in the congregation. We took two polls, the first of what skills were available, and the second of how many hours a week these men might be able to work on a church project. We were astonished: within our body was practically every building skill we would need—plumbers, electricians, carpenters, a stained-glass artisan, a mason, a construction supervisor—the list went on and on. All we would need, apparently, were funds for the materials.

But the most amazing part of this story happened

just five months after we had made our first down payment. In December of '77, right at Christmas time, our area was hit with a windstorm so severe that no one could remember ever seeing anything like it. Suddenly, according to two eyewitnesses, a ferocious gust seemed to rush up all sides of the mountain at once, and lifted the tepee straight up in the air, about a hundred feet. The wind didn't fling it apart, scattering debris all over the countryside. Instead the tepee seemed to hang in midair for one brief moment and then came crashing to earth, the wreckage landing exactly where it had stood.

The newspaper headline called it: AN ACT OF GOD.

If this book has been a blessing to you, please let me know. Each month I prepare Praise News in which I share new things that I learn about praise. I will be pleased to send this to you at no charge if you request it.

Write to:

Merlin R. Carothers
Box 2518
Escondido, CA 92025

The Foundation of Praise

is now supplying free copies of this book to:

PRISONS: Federal, state, county and many in foreign countries.

HOSPITALS: Civilian and Veterans'.

MILITARY: Bases throughout the United States and to our servicemen wherever stationed.

CRISIS PREGNANCY CENTERS: These books are saving lives.

NEEDY PEOPLE—world-wide.

You can help supply free books to those who desperately need help through your contributions to:

Foundation of Praise, Box 2518, Escondido, CA 92025

Other books by Merlin Carothers that you will want to read:

PRISON TO PRAISE
Merlin Carothers first book. This book has been printed in thirty-one languages and distributed in over sixty countries. Many people have reported transformed lives as a result of reading the powerful message found in this book.

POWER IN PRAISE
An in-depth study of the working and scriptural basis for the principle introduced in *Prison to Praise:* in all things give praise and thanks to God. Praising God in one's predicaments is first acknowledging that God is in control of everything, whether or not it is in His will, and that He has the power to turn all things to good. Secondly, the act of obediently praising God begins to soften our hearts and produces a right heart attitude — a prerequisite for any act of God.

ANSWERS TO PRAISE
The proof of the pudding! No sooner did the first two Praise books come out than the phone calls and letters started pouring in. Praise works! Overjoyed Christians felt compelled to share the "signs and wonders following" with the author, adding their own testimonies to the rapidly-growing record. Miracle upon miracle, from all walks of life!

PRAISE WORKS
More letters selected from an assortment of thousands illustrate the secret of *freedom through praise!* Includes a letter from Frank Foglio — (author of *Hey, God!*) — who learned the power of praise when his daughter recovered miraculously after 7 long years in the "hopeless" ward of an institution for the mentally ill. Other letters are from a nurse, a nun, an attorney, a blind girl, a chaplain, an alcoholic and many others! Praise for brain surgery, praise for prison, praise for the Lord!

WALKING AND LEAPING

When Merlin Carothers lost a new car and trailer, along with his most-prized possessions, in a freak traffic accident — he praised God. But when he found himself singlehandedly overseeing the construction of a massive church building with only the enthusiastic but unskilled labor of his parishioners, and with the precarious backing of a bank balance that generally registered zero, he had to learn to "praise God in all things" all over again. "Fascinating and exciting. I thoroughly enjoyed it."
— New Life Magazine

BRINGING HEAVEN INTO HELL

Now Merlin Carothers goes beyond his earlier works to explore life-changing situations which others have experienced. The author shares these discoveries of God's forgiveness, a new freedom in Christ and the power of the Holy Spirit to shed light from heaven in the midst of a personal hell.

THE BIBLE ON PRAISE

This beautifully-printed, four-color, thirty-two page booklet features selected verses on praise from thirty-eight books of the Bible. These are Merlin's favorite verses and were personally selected by him. This booklet makes a lovely gift with a message that will bless the reader for years.

MORE POWER TO YOU

Worldwide demand for more information on power has resulted in *More Power To You* — written for persons in everyday places who need more power in their everyday lives. Though presented in simple easy-to-read language, the author had given us profound and useful insights into serious problems of modern life. This book is a beautiful key to unlock a vast storehouse of spiritual power.

COMMENTS on Merlin Carothers' latest book, WHAT'S ON YOUR MIND?

THE WHITE HOUSE — Herb Ellingwood — *Legal Counsel to President Reagan:* "*What's on Your Mind?* is the best book I have read in years —for me and for the nation! Thanks for being receptive to God's message. Please send 100 copies. I believe this is what our governmental leaders need."

Two Months Later: "We are now using *What's on Your Mind?* in our weekly Bible study group."

ASTRONAUT — James Irwin — who walked on the moon: "Excellent! Courageous! Please send 30 copies."

PRESIDENT OF ASBURY THEOLOGICAL SEMINARY — David L. McKenna: "I have reviewed *What's on Your Mind?* Please send a copy for each of our forty faculty members."

EDITOR FOR CHOSEN BOOKS — David Manuel: "This will be the number one Christian book this year."

AUTHOR — Judson Cornwall: "It addresses a deep need. It is good!"

AD AGENCY VICE-PRESIDENT — Dick Meyers: "This is Merlin's best book."

PASTORS: "Every pastor in the world must read this book. I have read thousands of books, and this is the first time I have made such a statement."

"When I read *What's on Your Mind?* I felt as though God had a searchlight on my soul."

TEACHER: "The first book I have read that is pertinent and superb for teenagers and senior citizens."

LAYMEN: *"What's on Your Mind?"* set me free from a burden I had carried over 25 years. Every Christian in the world must read this book."

"This is the most unusual book I have read during my 35 years as a Christian."

ALSO AVAILABLE ON CASSETTE:

Merlin Carothers traces the practical uses of praise in all of his books - the simple application of Biblical truth: **all things work together for good. . .in everything give thanks. . .count it all joy.**
Like spiritual dynamite, praise has an explosive quality. Released in a life, it revolutionizes everything with which it comes in contact.

—NOTES—